KEVIN BARTLETT'S
BOOK OF
FOOTBALL

Stories • Statistics • Trivia

Compiled by Kevin Bartlett, AM

The Five Mile Press

With thanks to Channel 7 for its support for this project.

For all enquiries regarding Kevin Bartlett please contact:

Raceplay the Sporting Company
552 City Road
SOUTH MELBOURNE 3205

Tel: (03) 9 699 4188
Fax: (03) 9 690 9115

Foreword

Tommy Hafey said to me, 'You should look after Bartlett, he's a terrific fella, terrific.'

A meeting was arranged in August 1983 during the weeks leading up to Kevin's retirement, when it seemed the whole country was focusing on his football achievements — it was impossible to get away from 'KB': over four hundred games, no handballs and hundreds of goals.

It seemed obvious to me that I should bone up on footy history in preparation for our meeting. Who would want to be with one of the greats of all time and not be able to chat about who played on who in the such and such? I need not have concerned myself. We met over several cups of tea and the main topic was rock 'n roll. Ever since, he has taken great delight in reminding me of obscure humorous facts of our many dealings along the show biz highway together.

This journey has seen Kevin in all areas of the media. Hosting his own radio and television programmes, writing for newspapers, making many personal appearances around Australia, and specializing in corporate presentations. These days he heads his own footy broadcast team on Magic 693 and contributes to the exciting new *Sports Weekly* magazine. Between these commitments, he enjoys appearing on the highly acclaimed Channel 7 football telecasts and 'Sportsworld'.

He is delighted when I don't discuss football, but will ask me to repeat the stories about the painted piano, music tours of the 'sixties and eccentricities of certain drummers.

A dedicated family man, Kevin (or 'Johnny' as we like to call him sometimes now that he is in show biz) is never happier than when he is working on a new project. I just hope that he never writes a book on the rock 'n roll stories I have told him!

Kevin once reminded me that one day he was playing football, then he joined the media and became an expert, overnight! Of course, after reading this book, anyone can become an expert.

One of the highlights of a day is when Kevin calls by the office to see his daughter Cara, who now works with us at Raceplay. It never takes long before my partner Gary Gray is acting out jokes and stories while Kevin laughs till he cries.

Tommy Hafey is right!

DANNY FINLEY
Friend, partner
June 1995

Statistics

The statistics in this book have been drawn from many sources. The main reference was the *1995 AFL Media Guide*. Most statistics are yearly records, and as such are current to the end of the 1994 season. Other statistics, where possible, have been up-dated, and were current at the time of going to press in June 1995.

All care has been taken to ensure the accuracy of the statistics provided, but the Author and Publishers cannot be responsible for any unwitting error.

Abbreviations

The following abbreviations have been used frequently throughout the book. Other abbreviations are explained as they occur.

AFL:	Australian Football League
VFL:	Victorian Football League (which was re-named the Australian Football League in 1990)
League:	The VFL/AFL
Tribunal:	The VFL/AFL Tribunal
MCG:	Melbourne Cricket Ground
SCG:	Sydney Cricket Ground
WACA:	The Western Australia Cricket Ground
'Gabba:	Woolloongabba ground (Brisbane)
WAFL:	Western Australian Football League

Contents

The Australian Football League

The Australian Football League (AFL) was originally named the Victorian Football League (VFL). It was formed in Victoria immediately after the 1896 Victorian Football Association (VFA) season as a breakaway group.

The first round of VFL matches was played in May 1897.

The original eight clubs in the VFL were: Carlton, Collingwood, Essendon, Fitzroy, Geelong, Melbourne, St Kilda and South Melbourne.

In 1908, Richmond and University joined the competition, but University was to disband after the 1914 season.

In 1916, only Carlton, Collingwood, Fitzroy and Richmond competed due to World War I difficulties.

Geelong and South Melbourne re-joined the League in 1917, and Essendon and St Kilda followed suit in 1918. Melbourne re-entered in 1919.

In 1925, Footscray, Hawthorn and North Melbourne were admitted to the League.

During 1942 and 1943, Geelong did not field a team as a result of World War II restrictions.

South Melbourne moved to the Harbor City in 1982 and was renamed Sydney.

In 1987, Brisbane and West Coast were admitted to the League.

In 1990, the League became a national league and was renamed the Australian Football League (AFL).

Adelaide was admitted to the League in 1991, and Fremantle followed in 1995.

The Clubs

There are currently 16 clubs in the AFL. The numbers of competing teams in the League over the years since its formation in 1897 are as follows:

1897–1907:	8	1918:	8	1944–86:	12
1908–1914:	10	1919–24:	9	1987–90:	14
1915:	9	1925–41:	12	1991–94:	15
1916:	4	1942–43:	11	1995:	16
1917:	6				

Background information about each of the clubs is provided on the following pages.

CLUB	JOINED LEAGUE	HOME GROUND	CLUB COLOURS
Adelaide *Crows*	1991	Football Park (1991–)	Navy blue guernsey with red and gold hoops.
Brisbane *Bears*	1987	Carrara (1987-92) Woolloongabba (1991, 1993–)	Maroon guernsey with gold 'V' and white trim.
Carlton *Blues*	1897	Princes Park (1897–)	Navy blue guernsey with white monogram.
Collingwood *Magpies* *'Pies*	1897	Victoria Park (1897–) Melbourne Cricket Ground (1993–)	Vertical black and white striped guernsey
Essendon *Bombers* *'Dons*	1897	East Melbourne Cricket Ground (1897–1921) Windy Hill (1922–91) Melbourne Cricket Ground (1992–)	Black guernsey with red sash
Fitzroy *Lions*	1897	Brunswick St Oval (1897–1966) Princes Park (1967–69, 1987–1993) Junction Oval (1970–84) Victoria Park (1985–86) Western Oval (1993–)	Light maroon guernsey with royal blue yoke and trimmings with gold monogram and lion emblem.
Footscray *Bulldogs* *'Dogs*	1925	Western Oval (1925–41, 1943–) Yarraville (1942)	Blue guernsey with red and white bands
Fremantle *Dockers*	1995	Subiaco (1995–) Western Australia Cricket Ground (1995–)	Purple guernsey with green and red chest panels separated by a white anchor.
Geelong *Cats*	1897	Corio Oval (1897–1940) Kardinia Park (1941–)	Navy blue and white hooped guernsey

* *Italicised names under the club names denote the teams' most common nicknames.*

Hawthorn *Hawks*	1925	Glenferrie Oval (1925–73) Princes Park (1974–91) Waverley Park (1990–)	Vertical brown and gold striped guernsey.
Melbourne *Demons* *Redlegs*	1897	Melbourne Cricket Ground (1897–1941,1946–) Motordrome (1932) Punt Rd Oval (1942–46)	Navy blue guernsey with red yoke.
North Melbourne *Kangaroos* *'Roos*	1925	Arden St Oval (1925–64, 1966–85) Coburg (1965) Melbourne Cricket Ground (1984–)	Vertical royal blue and white striped guernsey.
Richmond *Tigers*	1908	Punt Rd Oval (1908–64) Melbourne Cricket Ground (1965–)	Black guernsey with gold sash.
St Kilda *Saints*	1897	Junction Oval (1897–1964) Toorak Park (1942–43) Moorabbin (1965–92) Waverley Park (1993–)	Vertical red, white and black striped guernsey with crest.
South Melbourne/ Sydney *Swans*	1897	Lake Oval (1897–1941,1947–81) Princes Park (1942–43) Junction Oval (1944–46) Sydney Cricket Ground (1982–)	White guernsey with red yoke incorporating opera house insignia and red back.
University *The Students*	1908	East Melbourne Cricket Ground (1908–10) Melbourne Cricket Ground (1911–14)	Black guernsey with blue 'V'
West Coast *Eagles*	1987	Subiaco (1987–) Western Australia Cricket Ground (1987–)	Blue guernsey with gold eagle wings incorporating emblem.

True Boots

The football public has always been fascinated by the champion goalkicker, for it is much more glamorous to kick goals than to save them. And full-forwards have always been the games biggest drawcards, for they are the heroes that attract the football public through the turnstiles. They have, on many occasions, been given movie star status.

To kick a hundred goals in a season is akin to making a century in Test cricket, and such a deed etches one's name into the history books. Kick 150 goals in a season, and you are guaranteed immortality. But aside from these great tallies, there are also the single goals that have captured the imagination, the unforgettable ones that have won premierships and saved a game after the siren. Our great game has many such great moments, as I hope the stories on the following pages show.

Lucky Demons

Melbourne supporters can thank Hassa Mann for the club winning the 1964 Grand Final. In the second last game of the season, Mann kicked a miracle goal in the dying moments to enable the Demons to snatch victory over Hawthorn by four points. Mann's kick was surely the most important of his great career. Had he missed, Melbourne would not have made the finals let alone take the flag. That kick from deep on the boundary line saw the Demons finish on top of the ladder and Hawthorn out of the finals in fifth position. Ironically, had Mann kicked a point, Hawthorn would have finished on top of the ladder and Melbourne would have finished fifth.

The Unforgettable Snap

No Carlton supporter will ever forget Freddy Stafford. After trailing all day in the 1947 Grand Final against Essendon, Carlton came good with ten minutes to play. A goal to Fred Davies left the Blues only 6 points down, but then came a string of heart stopping misses: Davies from 15 metres out failed to goal, then kicks from Ken Baxter and Ken Hands also failed to make the distance. With 40 seconds left, Baxter on the ground replacing injured Blues champion Bert Deacon came through hard in the ruck and the ball went to ground. Stafford pounced on the loose ball, and from 25 metres out put his left foot snap through the centre, giving the Blues the flag by one point.

A Century Missed

The last round of the 1990 season saw North Melbourne playing Collingwood at Waverley Park. The Kangaroos could not make the finals, but it was an important day for North's spearhead Johnny Longmire. Going into the game, Longmire had 96 goals pegged to his name for the season and only needed four goals to become the youngest player ever to kick 100 goals in League football. At 19 years of age he was about to rewrite the history books. Unfortunately for Longmire, he was off target and booted 2 goals 8 leaving him two short of the milestone and the record. No player in League history has come closer to kicking a century of goals and missing out. Several players have kicked 97 goals in a season, but never 98. Doug Wade and Malcolm Blight still remain the only North Melbourne players to kick a century of goals in a season.

The Kick that Killed a Hoodoo

Hawthorn joined the VFL in 1925 along with North Melbourne and Footscray, but it took until the 1960 season for the Hawks to beat

Collingwood at Victoria Park. During that period of time, Hawthorn had played and lost 28 matches at the Magpies' home ground. When Collingwood, who had trailed for most of the day, hit the front late in the last quarter it appeared the 'Pies had snatched victory yet again, but with only seconds to go the Hawks made one last charge and champion full-forward John Peck marked as the siren sounded. Peck calmly went back and kicked the historic goal that gave Hawthorn a one point win — 7 goals 16 (58) to 7 goals, 15 (57).

Premiership Boils Over

On the eve of the 1936 final series the Tribunal handed down a sensational sentence. The Tribunal found Collingwood champion Gordon Coventry guilty of striking Richmond defender Joe Murdoch and suspended him for eight weeks. Coventry, a veteran of 287 games, had never been reported in his career and he retaliated because Murdoch had struck him on the back of the neck. Murdoch's target was a massive boil on the neck of the Magpie star. Despite public meetings and newspaper condemnation of the Tribunal's actions, the judgement remained and Coventry missed playing in the Magpies' premiership side. Upset and disappointed, Coventry retired, but he was persuaded to play one more year before hanging up his boots as the game's record-holder with 306 games. He finally finished with 1299 goals, the most ever kicked in League football.

After the Siren

What Melbourne supporter could ever forget the 1987 Preliminary Final? With only seconds to go, the Demons led Hawthorn by 4 points and looked certain to play in their first grand final since 1964. The crowd was all for the underdog Demons and the noise reached fever pitch as Hawthorn made one last effort to save the match. And when champion half-forward Gary Buckenara marked, he appeared to be too far out to score. And then the unthinkable happened: Melbourne ruckman Jimmy Stynes infringed by running between Buckenara and the man on the mark. A 15-metre penalty was awarded, and the final siren sounded. Buckenara, regarded as the best kick in the side, then went back and to the horror of Demon's supporters, kicked the goal to snatch a 2-point victory for Hawthorn.

The Pop Star Sharpshooter

One must never underestimate the greatness of Collingwood champion full-forward Peter McKenna, although somehow the umpires overlooked this goal-kicking phenomenon when casting Brownlow medal votes. McKenna, with his mop-top Beatle haircut, created rock-star type hysteria during his playing days with the Magpies — and boy, could he play. Eight times he topped the Magpies' goal-kicking lists, and on three occasions kicked a century of goals. In 1970 he booted 143 goals but polled only 11 Brownlow votes. In 1971 he kicked 134 goals with just six votes, and in 1972, 130 goals for eight miserly votes. McKenna might not have won a Brownlow, but he did cut a record — a pop record which topped the charts at Victoria Park!

A Century at the MCG

Doug Wade, playing for North Melbourne in the last round of the 1974 season, posted a magnificent milestone against Hawthorn when he kicked his second goal of the match: He became only the second player in League history to kick 1000 career goals, equalling the effort of Collingwood great Gordon 'Nuts' Coventry. He also has the unique record of kicking 100 goals in a season with two League clubs. In 1969, the burly full-forward booted 127 goals for Geelong, and 103 goals for North Melbourne in 1974. Wade also has the unique record of kicking his 100th goal in a grand final — this was achieved in 1974 against Richmond.

The Eye of an Eagle

Peter Sumich has starred for the Eagles since his debut in 1989. In that season, he kicked 45 goals with the promise of more to come. The following year, 90 goals established him as one of the League's top sharpshooters, rivalling Hawthorn's Jason Dunstall and Sydney Swans' (formerly St Kilda's) Tony Lockett. A century of goals came in 1991, but not even 111 majors for the year could give the Eagles the flag — they went down to Hawthorn. But that year Sumich set a club record when he kicked 13 goals against Footscray, and he also set a League record for the most goals kicked in a game by a left-footer. He became the only left-footer to kick 100 goals in a season.

Going Out on Top

The last game of the 1991 season provided a fairytale ending to the career of David Cloke. 'Clokey' returned home to his former club Richmond in 1990 after a seven-year stay at Collingwood. Cloke, in his last hurrah and in his mid-thirties, lined up against Carlton in the ruck but was moved to the forward pocket before quarter time. In fact, just before quarter time, it was suggested in the coach's box (because I was coaching Richmond on that particular day) that maybe Cloke should be taken from the field because Justin Madden was far too tall for him. But because it was Cloke's last day of League football, I felt it was inappropriate to take him from the field, hence I put him down into the forward pocket. He immediately kicked two goals and proceeded to mesmerize the Carlton defence, kicking eight goals for the match. At 36 years of age and carrying a fair amount of cellulite, Cloke had kicked his biggest bag of goals ever in a League game, and in fact finished with a career game tally of 333 games, as well as a career goal tally of 333.

Just One More Goal...

In 1940, Collingwood star full-forward Ron Todd shocked the Magpies when he agreed to play for Williamstown in the VFA. Todd, in only 83 games, had booted 227 goals, including a record 23 goals in the 1939 finals series. The VFL promptly disqualified Todd for five years for crossing over without a clearance. Todd didn't let his fans down. He booted 672 goals in just 140 games for Williamstown in an awesome display of his freakish ability. Todd retired in 1949 with one regret: His VFL/VFA goal tally stood at 999 goals — one short of a fabulous milestone.

Sharpshooter's Tragedy

The season in 1972 started with a bombshell when Hawk star Peter Hudson went down in the opening game against Melbourne with a serious knee injury. Hudson, who had already booted eight of Hawthorn's nine goals in a classic display at full-forward, was carried from the field and missed the rest of the season. The year before, Hudson had equalled Bob Pratt's record of 150 goals in spearheading the Hawks to their second flag. Without Hudson, Hawthorn could only finish sixth and missed the finals.

The Comeback Kid

Round 21 of the 1973 season saw the dramatic return to League football of Peter Hudson. The Hawks champion had been sidelined since the opening game of the 1972 season with a knee injury. Needing to win to find a place in the finals, Hawthorn surprised the football world by including Hudson in their line-up. In an appearance befitting a Hollywood star, Hudson arrived at Waverley in a helicopter. Overweight and slow, Hudson lined himself in the goal square, and virtually never moved from the goal square all day. But, the legend was back, and Hudson didn't let his admirers down, booting eight goals as he mesmerized the Magpies' defence. At one stage, the Magpies' full-back was even facing Hudson and not even looking at the game. Hudson had completely demoralised Collingwood's team. But even the magic of Hudson couldn't stop Collingwood winning the game by 18 points, and Hawthorn missed the finals for the second year in a row.

A Dozen and a Half

Records are made to be broken, so the saying goes. But Fred Fanning's record of kicking 18 goals in a League game for Melbourne still defies the League's greatest sharpshooters today. Fanning kicked 18 goals 1 in the last game of the 1947 season against St Kilda at the Junction Oval. Ironically, it was his last game of League football. The week before he had kicked 10 goals against Footscray, giving him 28 goals in his last two League games. Fanning finished the season with 97 goals, still the highest number of goals kicked by a Melbourne player in a season.

Just Falling Short

Round 7 of the 1992 season saw one of the game's great League goal-kicking records under threat. Hawthorn's Jason Dunstall had bagged 12 goals up to half-time at Waverley against Richmond. Fred Fanning's League record of 18 goals for Melbourne against St Kilda in 1947 looked certain to fall, but at the day's end, Dunstall had to settle for 17, one short of a fabulous mark. Dunstall did, however, create a Hawthorn club record, beating the previous best, which was 16 goals by Peter Hudson. Also, in kicking 17 goals, Dunstall created a new Waverley Park record, which still stands.

Welcome to the Big League

Round 1 of 1949 saw the making of a legend. John Coleman, a new recruit from Hastings, lined up for the Bombers as full-forward against Hawthorn at Windy Hill. His opponent that day was Fred Wain, who was also making his debut for Hawthorn. For Wain, it wasn't a memorable game; for Coleman, it was. He booted 12 goals, equalling the record for the most number of goals kicked in an opening game, which was held by another Essendon spearhead, Ted Freyer. Coleman's 12 goals still remain a record on debut. Coleman also in his debut year booted 100 goals, with his century of goals coming up in the Bombers' grand final win against Carlton. Essendon players went out of their way once the game was all but won to ensure that Coleman kicked his century of goals. At times, they even kicked the ball backwards, so they could keep possession in their attempts to get the ball to Coleman. John Coleman is still the only player to kick 100 goals in his first season of League football.

Opposite page: Jason Dunstall of Hawthorn shoots for goal in the Round 22 match against Essendon in 1994. (John Daniels/Sporting Pix)

True Boot

Collingwood sharpshooter Peter McKenna is regarded by many as the most accurate kick of a goal in League history. From Round 1 of 1968 to Round 4 in 1974 he managed to kick at least one goal in each of the 120 matches that he played. No other League player has managed as many consecutive goalscoring appearances.

A Baker's Dozen

Champion Adelaide full-forward Tony Modra created League history in the opening game of the 1994 season. Modra, who has had an eventful career, booted 13 goals against Carlton at Football Park. In doing so, the highflying full-forward created an opening goalkicking record, surpassing the previous record held by Ted Freyer of Essendon, John Coleman of Essendon, Peter McKenna of Collingwood, and Jason Dunstall of Hawthorn. Modra also equalled his previously best goalkicking record of 13 goals, which was booted against Richmond in 1993.

Quick Draw Jako

In 1991, Melbourne's colourful full-forward Allen Jakovich created a new goalkicking record. Jakovich scored his 50th career goal in only his ninth game, reaching the half-century faster than any player in the game's history. Four other players have kicked 50 goals in their first ten games, they being Alan Rait of Footscray in 1937, John Coleman of Essendon in 1949, Ross Ditchburn for Carlton in 1982, and Adrian McAdam for North Melbourne in 1993. But no-one has done it quicker than Jakovich in just nine games.

Never the Two Flags

Magpie centre half-back Ted Potter never once troubled the goal umpires. He played 182 matches from 1963 to '72 and holds the record for remaining goalless throughout a long career. Geelong champion full-back Gary Malarkey came closer to Potter than any other player when he failed to cause a goal umpire to raise two flags in any of his 172 matches between 1977 and '86.

One-man Team

Arthur Best may well have wondered whether he was playing the opposition on his own when he played a memorable last League match for Melbourne against South Melbourne at the Lake Oval on 29 August 1914. Best registered his team's entire score of 5 goals and 5 behinds. Despite his great effort, the Southerners won by 43 points.

Daddy of them All

Collingwood's Gordon 'Nuts' Coventry scored a career record total of 1299 goals in 306 matches between 1920 and 1937. He scored more than 100 majors against all but one opposition club. Footscray's defence held him to 89 goals in the 16 matches that he played against them. On 63 occasions, he managed 7 goals or more in a League match.

The Time Machines

Champion full-forward Harry 'Soapy' Vallence of Carlton and Peter Hudson of Hawthorn share the honour of being the most durable of the ten-goals-in-a-match brigade. Vallence kicked 11 goals against South Melbourne at the Lake Oval in Round 15 in 1929. Exactly nine years later he managed to boot the same tally against Fitzroy at the Brunswick Street Oval. Hudson kicked his first bag of 10 when the Hawks lost to Essendon at Windy Hill in the opening round of 1968. In Round 17, 1977, he booted ten goals against St Kilda at Waverley Park.

Goals, Goals, and More Goals

South Melbourne superstar Bob Pratt provided the greatest five-match individual goalscoring avalanche in League history 61 years ago. From Round 11 to Round 15 in 1934 the highflying full-forward registered tallies of 9, 8, 11, 11, and 12 goals, giving him a total of 51 goals in five games.

There's Life in the Old Dog Yet!

The oldest player to kick ten goals or more in a League game was St Kilda's Dave McNamara. McNamara was 35 years and 230 days old when he scored 10 goals from 12 shots against Geelong at the Junction Oval in Round 17, 1922. Nine of his successful shots were place kicks. He also hit the post once.

Not Just your Average Bloke...

Jack McMillan is not a household name when it comes to star full-forwards, despite being recruited from Hastings, the same club as the legendary John Coleman, to play for Footscray in 1936. In fact, McMillan played only four matches during his only League season. However, his career tally of 17 goals does put him up there with the superstars. His goals per match average of 4.25 has been bettered only by nine men in almost 100 years. During that time, around 10 000 players have played VFL/AFL football.

The Half-century Club

It's rare for three players from the same club to score 50 goals or more in a particular season. Four clubs, Melbourne, Richmond, Hawthorn and North Melbourne, are the only clubs to record such an achievement. This first happened in 1926 for Melbourne, when Harry Moyes booted 55 goals, Bob Johnson snr, 51, and Harry Davie, 50. It then took until 1971 for Richmond, to produce Royce Hart, 77 goals, Kevin Bartlett, 53 goals and Barry Richardson 50 goals, and again in 1972 with the Richmond trio Neil Balme, 55 goals, Ricky McLean, 55 goals, and Rex Hunt, 51. Then in 1977, Hawthorn produced Peter Hudson with 110 goals, Leigh Matthews with 91 goals and John Hendrie with 53 goals. Again it was the Hawks in 1984. This time Leigh Matthews with 77 goals, Ken Judge with 63 and Dermott Brereton with 50. And then in 1993, North Melbourne produced John Longmire with 75 goals, Adrian McAdam with 68 goals and Wayne Carey with 64 goals.

Magic Milestones

Teams love to celebrate the occasion of a player registering his 100th goal in a season. The following champions have excelled by registering 10 goals or more on the day their century was reached. Gordon Coventry first did it for Collingwood when he booted ten goals against Melbourne at Victoria Park in Round 18 in 1933. The great Bob Pratt of South Melbourne booted 11 goals against Carlton at the Lake Oval in Round 13 of 1934. Geelong's champion Doug Wade also booted 11 goals against Footscray at Kardinia Park in Round 16 of 1969. Then Peter Hudson did it for Hawthorn when he kicked 11 goals against Footscray at Waverley Park in Round 16 of 1970. Tony Lockett, while playing for St Kilda, booted 10 goals against Adelaide at Football Park in Round 22 of 1991. And the great Gary Ablett of Geelong also booted ten goals against North Melbourne at the MCG in Round 18, 1993.

Opposite page: Tony Lockett, playing for St Kilda against Hawthorn, kicks a goal in Round 22 of the 1994 AFL season. (John Daniels/Sporting Pix)

• Quick Quiz •

1 Who was the first League player to score 100 goals in a season?

2 How many goals did John Coleman kick in his first match for Essendon?

3 Who scored 18 goals in his last League match?

4 Name the first player to score a goal in a League match at Carrara.

5 Which League player scored 10 or more goals in three successive matches during 1934?

6 Who kicked the first goal in AFL football for:

West Coast?
Adelaide?
Brisbane?
Fremantle?

7 Three players have kicked exactly 100 goals in an AFL season. Name them.

8 Who kicked 134 goals in a season but did not head the League goalkicking tally for that year?

9 Who has kicked the greatest aggregate number of goals for Melbourne?

10 Apart from Stephen Kernahan, name the last player to head the goalkicking at Carlton.

Answers

1   *Gordon Coventry, Collingwood.*

2   *Twelve.*

3   *Fred Fanning, Melbourne.*

4   *Doug Barwick, Fitzroy.*

5   *Bob Pratt, South Melbourne.*

6   *Laurie Keene, Tony McGuinness, Bernie Harris, Todd Ridley.*

7   *Jack Titus (1940, Richmond), John Coleman (1949, Essendon), Brian Taylor (1986, Collingwood).*

8   *Peter McKenna (1971, Collingwood).*

9   *Norm Smith (546 goals, 1935–1948).*

10   *Mark Maclure (48 goals, 1985).*

LEADING GOALKICKERS INCLUDING FINALS 1897–1994

Year	No.	Name	Club
1897	27	James, Eddy	Geelong
1898	31	Smith, Archie	Collingwood
1899	31	James, Eddy	Geelong
1900	26	Thurgood, Albert	Essendon
1901	34	Hiskins, Fred	Essendon
1902	33	Rowell, Ted	Collingwood
1903	35	Lockwood, Ted	Collingwood
1904	39	Coutie, A. Vin	Melbourne
1905	38	Pannam, Charlie	Collingwood
1906	50	Grace, Mick	Carlton
1907	47	Lee, Dick	Collingwood
1908	54	Lee, Dick	Collingwood
1909	58	Lee, Dick	Collingwood
1910	58	Lee, Dick	Collingwood
1911	47	Gardiner, Vin	Carlton
1912	56	Brereton, Harry	Melbourne
1913	56	Freake, Jim	Fitzroy
1914	57	Lee, Dick	Collingwood
1915	66	Lee, Dick	Collingwood
	66	Freake, Jim	Fitzroy
1916	48	Lee, Dick	Collingwood
1917	54	Lee, Dick	Collingwood
1918	34	Cowley, Ern	Carlton
1919	56	Lee, Dick	Collingwood
1920	63	Bayliss, George	Richmond
1921	64	Lee, Dick	Collingwood
1922	56	Clover, Horrie	Carlton
1923	68	Stockdale, Greg	Essendon
1924	82	Moriarty, Jack	Fitzroy
1925	78	Hagger, Lloyd	Geelong
1926	83	Coventry, Gordon	Collingwood
1927	97	Coventry, Gordon	Collingwood
1928	89	Coventry, Gordon	Collingwood
1929	124	Coventry, Gordon	Collingwood
1930	119	Coventry, Gordon	Collingwood
1931	86	Vallence, Harry	Carlton
1932	109	Moloney, George	Geelong
1933	109	Pratt, Bob	South Melbourne
1934	150	Pratt, Bob	South Melbourne
1935	103	Pratt, Bob	South Melbourne
1936	101	Mohr, Bill	St Kilda
1937	72	Coventry, Gordon	Collingwood
1938	120	Todd, Ron	Collingwood
1939	121	Todd, Ron	Collingwood

LEADING GOALKICKERS (cont.)

1940	100	Titus, Jack	Richmond
1941	88	Smith, Norm	Melbourne
1942	80	White, Lindsay	South Melbourne
1943	62	Harris, Dick	Richmond
	62	Fanning, Fred	Melbourne
1944	87	Fanning, Fred	Melbourne
1945	67	Fanning, Fred	Melbourne
1946	66	Brittingham, Bill	Essendon
1947	97	Fanning, Fred	Melbourne
1948	86	White, Lindsay	Geelong
1949	100	Coleman, John	Essendon
1950	120	Coleman, John	Essendon
1951	86	Goninon, George	Geelong
1952	103	Coleman, John	Essendon
1953	97	Coleman, John	Essendon
1954	84	Collins, Jack	Footscray
1955	80	Rayson, Noel	Geelong
1956	56	Young, Bill	St Kilda
1957	74	Collins, Jack	Footscray
1958	73	Brewer, Ian	Collingwood
1959	68	Evans, Ron	Essendon
1960	67	Evans, Ron	Essendon
1961	54	Carroll, Tom	Carlton
1962	68	Wade, Doug	Geelong
1963	75	Peck, John	Hawthorn
1964	69	Peck, John	Hawthorn
1965	56	Peck, John	Hawthorn
1966	76	Fordham, Ted	Essendon
1967	96	Wade, Doug	Geelong
1968	125	Hudson, Peter	Hawthorn
1969	127	Wade, Doug	Geelong
1970	146	Hudson, Peter	Hawthorn
1971	150	Hudson, Peter	Hawthorn
1972	130	McKenna, Peter	Collingwood
1973	84	McKenna, Peter	Collingwood
1974	103	Wade, Doug	North Melbourne
1975	68	Matthews, Leigh	Hawthorn
1976	105	Donohue, Larry	Geelong
1977	110	Hudson, Peter	Hawthorn
1978	118	Templeton, Kelvin	Footscray
1979	91	Templeton, Kelvin	Footscray
1980	112	Roach, **Michael**	Richmond
1981	86	Roach, **Michael**	Richmond
1982	103	Blight, Malcolm	North Melbourne
1983	116	Quinlan, Bernie	Fitzroy
1984	105	Quinlan, Bernie	Fitzroy

LEADING GOALKICKERS (cont.)

1985	105	Beasley, Simon	Footscray
1986	100	Taylor, Brian	Collingwood
1987	117	Lockett, Tony	St Kilda
1988	132	Dunstall, Jason	Hawthorn
1989	138	Dunstall, Jason	Hawthorn
1990	98	Longmire, John	North Melbourne
1991	127	Lockett, Tony	St Kilda
1992	145	Dunstall, Jason	Hawthorn
1993	129	Modra, Tony	Adelaide
1994	129	Ablett, Gary	Geelong

MOST GOALS IN A MATCH

No.	Year	Name and Match
18	1947	Fanning, F. (Melbourne) v St Kilda
17	1930	Coventry, G. (Collingwood) v Fitzroy
17	1992	Dunstall, J. (Hawthorn) v Richmond
16	1929	Coventry, G. (Collingwood) v Hawthorn
16	1969	McKenna, P. (Collingwood) v South Melbourne
16	1969	Hudson, P. (Hawthorn) v Melbourne
15	1933	Coventry, G. (Collingwood) v Essendon
15	1934	Pratt, R. (South Melbourne) v Essendon
15	1978	Templeton, K. (Footscray) v St Kilda
15	1992	Lockett, T. (St Kilda) v Sydney
14	1931	Strang, D. (Richmond) v North Melbourne
14	1934	Coventry, G. (Collingwood) v Hawthorn
14	1954	Coleman, J. (Essendon) v Fitzroy
14	1989	Ablett, G. (Geelong) v Richmond
14	1990	Longmire, J. (North Melbourne) v Melbourne
14	1993	Ablett, G. (Geelong) v Essendon
14	1994	Ablett, G. (Geelong) v Sydney
13	1921	Clover, H. (Carlton) v St Kilda
13	1925	Davie, H. (Melbourne) v Carlton
13	1952	Coleman, J. (Essendon) v Geelong
13	1952	Coleman, J. (Essendon) v Hawthorn
13	1967	Wade, D. (Geelong) v South Melbourne
13	1969	Hudson, P. (Hawthorn) v South Melbourne
13	1970	Hudson, P. (Hawthorn) v South Melbourne
13	1971	Wade, D. (Geelong) v North Melbourne
13	1972	McKenna, P. (Collingwood) v Essendon
13	1991	Daicos, P. (Collingwood) v Brisbane
13	1991	Lockett, T. (St Kilda) v Carlton
13	1991	Sumich, P. (West Coast) v Footscray
13	1993	Modra, T. (Adelaide) v Richmond
13	1994	Modra, T. (Adelaide) v Carlton

GOALKICKING RECORDS AT AFL VENUES
MOST IN A MATCH

Carrara	13	Peter Daicos (Collingwood) v Brisbane	1991
Football Park	13	Tony Modra (Adelaide) v Richmond	1993
	13	Tony Modra (Adelaide) v Carlton	1994
Gabba	11	Billy Brownless (Geelong) v Brisbane	1991
Kardinia Park	13	Doug Wade (Geelong) v North Melbourne	1971
MCG	14	Gary Ablett (Geelong) v Richmond	1989
	14	Gary Ablett (Geelong) v Essendon	1993
	14	John Longmire (North Melbourne) v Melbourne	1990
Moorabbin	15	Tony Lockett (St Kilda) v Sydney	1992
North Hobart	8	Tony Lockett (St Kilda) v Fitzroy	1991
Princes Park	13	Harry Davie (Melbourne) v Carlton	1925
SCG	12	Brian Taylor (Collingwood) v Sydney	1985
Subiaco Oval	8	Peter Sumich (West Coast) v Footscray	1989
	8	Peter Sumich (West Coast) v Sydney	1990
	8	Tony Lockett (St Kilda) v West Coast	1991
	8	Darren Bewick (Essendon) v West Coast	1993
Victoria Park	17	Gordon Coventry (Collingwood) v Fitzroy	1930
WACA	13	Peter Sumich (West Coast) v Footscray	1991
Waverley Park	17	Jason Dunstall (Hawthorn) v Richmond	1992
Western Oval	15	Kelvin Templeton (Footscray) v St Kilda	1978
Windy Hill	14	John Coleman (Essendon) v Fitzroy	1954

MOST IN A CAREER

Carrara	107	Brad Hardie (Brisbane)	1987-91
Football Park	80	Tony Modra (Adelaide)	1992-94
Gabba	51	Roger Merrett (Brisbane)	1991-94
Kardinia Park	413	Doug Wade (Geelong/North Melbourne)	1961-75
MCG	380	Kevin Bartlett (Richmond)	1965-83
Moorabbin	329	Tony Lockett (St Kilda)	1983-92
North Hobart	12	Darren Wheildon (Fitzroy)	1991-92
Princes Park	357	Harry Vallence (Carlton)	1926-38
SCG	176	Warwick Capper (Sydney/Brisbane)	1983-91
Subiaco Oval	128	Peter Sumich (West Coast)	1989-94
Victoria Park	675	Gordon Coventry (Collingwood)	1920-37
WACA	80	Peter Sumich (West Coast)	1989-94
Waverley Park	354	Jason Dunstall (Hawthorn)	1985-94
Western Oval	219	Kelvin Templeton (Footscray/Melbourne)	1974-85
	219	Simon Beasley (Footscray)	1982-89
Windy Hill	282	John Coleman (Essendon)	1949-54

100 GOALS IN A SEASON

Year	Name	Club	No.
1934	Pratt, Bob	South Melbourne	150
1971	Hudson, Peter	Hawthorn	150
1970	Hudson, Peter	Hawthorn	146
1992	Dunstall, Jason	Hawthorn	145
1970	McKenna, Peter	Collingwood	143
1989	Dunstall, Jason	Hawthorn	138
1971	McKenna, Peter	Collingwood	134
1981	Dunstall, Jason	Hawthorn	132
1992	Lockett, Tony	St Kilda	132
1972	McKenna, Peter	Collingwood	130
1993	Modra, Tony	Adelaide	129
1994	Ablett, Gary	Geelong	129
1969	Wade, Doug	Geelong	127
1991	Lockett, Tony	St Kilda	127
1968	Hudson, Peter	Hawthorn	125
1929	Coventry, Gordon	Collingwood	124
1993	Ablett, Gary	Geelong	124
1993	Dunstall, Jason	Hawthorn	123
1939	Todd, Richard	Collingwood	121
1939	Todd, Richard	Collingwood	120
1950	Coleman, John	Essendon	120
1969	Hudson, Peter	Hawthorn	120
1930	Coventry, Gordon	Collingwood	119
1978	Templeton, Kelvin	Footscray	118
1987	Lockett, Tony	St Kilda	117
1983	Quinlan, Bernie	Fitzroy	116
1970	Jesaulenko, Alex	Carlton	115
1980	Roach, Michael	Richmond	112
1991	Sumich, Peter	West Coast	111
1977	Hudson, Peter	Hawthorn	110
1932	Moloney, George	Geelong	109
1933	Pratt, Bob	South Melbourne	109
1933	Coventry, Gordon	Collingwood	108
1972	Blethyn, Geoff	Essendon	107
1934	Coventry, Gordon	Collingwood	105
1976	Donohue, Larry	Geelong	105
1984	Quinlan, Bernie	Fitzroy	105
1984	Beasley, Simon	Footscray	105
1935	Pratt, Bob	South Melbourne	103
1952	Coleman, John	Essendon	103
1974	Wade, Doug	North Melbourne	103
1982	Blight, Macolm	North Melbourne	103
1987	Capper, Warwick	Sydney	103
1936	Mohr, Bill	St Kilda	101
1994	Dunstall, Jason	Hawthorn	101

100 GOALS IN A SEASON (cont.)

1940	Titus, Jack	Richmond	100
1949	Coleman, John	Essendon	100
1986	Taylor, Brian	Collingwood	100

OPENING ROUND GOALS

No.	Name	Club	Year
13	Tony Modra	(Adelaide) v Carlton	1994
12	Ted Freyer	(Essendon) v Melbourne	1935
12	John Coleman	(Essendon) v Hawthorn	1949
12	Peter McKenna	(Collingwood) v Hawthorn	1966
12	Jason Dunstall	(Hawthorn) v Geelong	1990
12	Jason Dunstall	(Hawthorn) v Geelong	1992
11	Leigh Matthews	(Hawthorn) v Melbourne	1981
11	Simon Beasley	(Footscray) v Richmond	1984

MOST GOALS ROUND BY ROUND

Round	No.	Name	Club	Year
Round 1	13	Tony Modra	(Adelaide) v Carlton	1994
Round 2	14	Doug Strang	(Richmond) v North Melbourne	1931
Round 3	15	Bob Pratt	(South Melbourne) v Essendon	1934
Round 4	12	Tony Lockett	(St Kilda) v Melbourne	1987
Round 5	16	Peter Hudson	(Hawthorn) v Melbourne	1969
Round 6	14	Gary Ablett	(Geelong) v Essendon	1993
Round 7	17	Jason Dunstall	(Hawthorn) v Richmond	1992
Round 8	13	John Coleman	(Essendon) v Geelong	1952
	13	Peter Hudson	(Hawthorn) v South Melbourne	1970
Round 9	14	Gary Ablett	(Geelong) v Richmond	1989
Round 10	11	Lindsay White	(Geelong) v St Kilda	1948
	11	Gary Ablett	(Geelong) v Brisbane	1988
Round 11	15	Gordon Coventry	(Collingwood) v Essendon	1933
Round 12	17	Gordon Coventry	(Collingwood) v Fitzroy	1930
Round 13	16	Gordon Coventry	(Collingwood) v Hawthorn	1934
Round 14	14	Gordon Coventry	(Collingwood) v Hawthorn	1934
	14	John Longmire	(North Melbourne) v Melbourne	1990
Round 15	12	Bob Pratt	(South Melbourne) v Footscray	1934
	12	Peter Hudson	(Hawthorn) v St Kilda	1971
	12	Simon Beasley	(Footscray) v Melbourne	1985
Round 16	13	Tony Modra	(Adelaide) v Richmond	1993
Round 17	13	Doug Wade	(Geelong) v South Melbourne	1967
Round 18	13	John Coleman	(Essendon) v Hawthorn	1952
Round 19	18	Fred Fanning	(Melbourne) v St Kilda	1947

MOST GOALS ROUND BY ROUND (cont.)

Round 20	13	Doug Wade	(Geelong) v North Melbourne	1971
	13	Peter Daicos	(Collingwood) v Brisbane	1991
Round 21	13	Tony Lockett	(St Kilda) v Carlton	1991
Round 22	11	Peter Hudson	(Hawthorn) v Fitzroy	1970
	11	Jason Dunstall	(Hawthorn) v St Kilda	1989
Round 23	11	Scott Hodges	(Adelaide) v Geelong	1992
Round 24	11	Tony Lockett	(St Kilda) v Sydney	1991

ALL-TIME TOP 10 GOALKICKERS

Gordon Coventry Collingwood Total No. of Goals: 1299

1920:	13	1926:	83	1932:	82
1921:	19	1927:	97	1933:	108
1922:	42	1928:	89	1934:	105
1923:	36	1929:	124	1935:	87
1924:	28	1930:	119	1936:	60
1925:	68	1931:	67	1937:	72

Doug Wade Geelong & North Melbourne Total No. of Goals: 1057

1961:	51	1967:	96	Transferred to	
1962:	68	1968:	64	North Melbourne	
1963:	48	1969:	127	1973:	73
1964:	41	1970:	74	1974:	103
1965:	29	1971:	94	1975:	47
1966:	52	1972:	90		

Jason Dunstall Hawthorn Total No. of Goals: 1011

1985:	36	1989:	138	1993:	123
1986:	77	1990:	83	1994:	101
1987:	94	1991:	82		
1988:	132	1992:	145		

Jack Titus Richmond Total No. of Goals: 970

1926:	1	1933:	42	1940:	100
1927:	0	1934:	80	1941:	87
1928:	26	1935:	83	1942:	67
1929:	54	1936:	83	1943:	24
1930:	50	1937:	65		
1931:	47	1938:	72		
1932:	41	1939:	48		

Leigh Matthews Hawthorn Total No. of Goals: 915

1969:	7	1975:	68	1981:	48
1970:	20	1976:	71	1982:	74
1971:	43	1977:	91	1983:	79
1972:	45	1978:	71	1984:	77
1973:	51	1979:	30	1985:	56
1974:	52	1980:	32		

ALL-TIME TOP 10 GOALKICKERS (cont.)

Tony Lockett St Kilda Total No. of Goals: 898

1983:	19	1987:	117	1991:	127
1984:	77	1988:	35	1992:	132
1985:	79	1989:	78	1993:	53
1986:	60	1990:	65	1994	56

Peter McKenna Collingwood & Carlton Total No. of Goals: 874

1965:	21	1970:	143	1975:	26
1966:	20	1971:	134	1976: Played in	
1967:	47	1972:	130	Tasmania	
1968:	64	1973:	86	Transferred to Carlton	
1969:	98	1974:	69	1977:	36

Gary Ablett Hawthorn & Geelong Total No. of Goals: 839

1982:	9	1987:	53	1992:	72
Transferred to Geelong		1988:	82	1993:	124
1984:	33	1989:	87	1994:	129
1985:	82	1990:	75		
1986:	65	1991:	28		

Bernie Quinlan Footscray & Fitzroy Total No. of Goals: 815

1969:	18	1976:	33	1982:	53
1970:	12	1977:	27	1983:	116
1971:	48	Transferred to Fitzroy		1984:	105
1972:	36	1978:	18	1985:	84
1973:	20	1979:	48	1986:	52
1974:	9	1980:	27		
1975:	36	1981:	73		

Kevin Bartlett Richmond Total No. of Goals: 778

1965:	13	1972:	34	1979:	36
1966:	19	1973:	31	1980:	84
1967:	38	1974:	47	1981:	58
1968:	38	1975:	42	1982:	58
1969:	30	1976:	27	1983:	37
1970:	34	1977:	55		
1971:	53	1978:	44		

Bill Mohr St Kilda Total No. of Goals: 736

1929:	40	1934:	66	1939:	47
1930:	83	1935:	83	1940:	25
1931:	57	1936:	101	1941:	1
1932:	67	1937:	58		
1933:	74	1938:	34		

Peter Hudson Hawthorn Total No. of Goals: 727

1967:	57	1970:	146	1973:	3
1968:	125	1971:	150	1974:	3
1969:	120	1972:	8	1977:	110

Harry Vallence Carlton Total No. of Goals: 722

1926:	19	1931:	86	1936:	86
1927:	25	1932:	97	1937:	39
1928:	22	1933:	84	1938:	81
1929:	64	1934:	35		
1930:	18	1935:	66		

ALL-TIME TOP 10 GOALKICKERS (cont.)

Dick Lee Collingwood Total No. of Goals: 707

1906:	35	1912:	2	1918:	17
1907:	47	1913:	8	1919:	56
1908:	54	1914:	57	1920:	20
1909:	58	1915:	66	1921:	64
1910:	58	1916:	48	1922:	38
1911:	25	1917:	54		

COLEMAN MEDALLISTS
HOME-AND-AWAY MATCHES ONLY

Name	Club	Total Goals	Year
Roach, Michael	Richmond	86	1981
Blight, Malcolm	North Melbourne	94	1982
Quinlan, Bernie	Fitzroy	106	1983
Quinlan, Bernie	Fitzroy	102	1984
Beasley, Simon	Footscray	93	1985
Taylor, Brian	Collingwood	100	1986
Lockett, Tony	St Kilda	117	1987
Dunstall, Jason	Hawthorn	124	1988
Dunstall, Jason	Hawthorn	126	1989
Longmire, John	North Melbourne	98	1990
Lockett, Tony	St Kilda	118	1991
Dunstall, Jason	Hawthorn	139	1992
Ablett, Gary	Geelong	124	1993
Ablett, Gary	Geelong	113	1994

The John Coleman Medal is awarded to the player who kicks the most goals in the home and away series.

CAREER GOALS TO 1994

Name	Games	Total Goals	Av. Goals per Game
Coventry, G. (Collingwood)	306	1299	4.25
Wade, D. (Geelong-North Melbourne)	267	1057	3.96
Titus, J. (Richmond)	294	970	3.30
Matthews, L. (Hawthorn)	332	915	2.76
Dunstall, J. (Hawthorn)	208	1011	4.86
McKenna, P. (Collingwood-Carlton)	191	874	4.58
Lockett, T. (St Kilda-Sydney)	183	898	4.91
Quinlan, B. (Footscray-Fitzroy)	366	815	2.23
Bartlett, K. (Richmond)	403	778	1.93
Mohr, W. (St Kilda)	195	736	3.77
Hudson, P. (Hawthorn)	129	727	5.64
Vallence, H. (Carlton)	204	722	3.54

CAREER GOALS TO 1994 (cont.)

Ablett, G. (Hawthorn-Geelong)	209	839	4.01
Lee, W. (Collingwood)	230	707	3.07
Pratt, R. (South Melbourne)	158	681	4.31
Moriarty, J. (Fitzroy-Essendon)	170	662	3.89
Moncrieff, M. (Hawthorn)	224	629	2.81
Roach, M. (Richmond)	200	607	3.03
Templeton, K. (Footscray-Melbourne)	177	593	3.35
Beasley, S. (Footscray)	154	575	3.73
Madden, S. (Essendon)	378	575	1.52
Smith, N. (Melbourne-Fitzroy)	228	572	2.51
Harris, R. (Richmond)	196	550	2.81
Daicos, P. (Collingwood)	250	549	2.20
White, L. (Geelong-South Melbourne)	144	542	3.76
Coleman, J. (Essendon)	98	537	5.48
Taylor, B. (Richmond-Collingwood)	140	527	3.76
Kernahan, S. (Carlton)	199	596	2.99
Hutchison, W. (Essendon)	290	496	1.71
Peck, J. (Hawthorn)	212	475	2.25
Spencer, J. (North Melbourne)	153	475	3.10
Forbes, K. (Essendon-North Melbourne-Fitzroy)	187	475	2.54
Daniher, T. (South Melbourne-Essendon)	313	470	1.50
Pannam, A. (Collingwood-Richmond)	183	461	2.52
Murray, S. (North Melbourne-Richmond)	121	457	3.78
Salmon, P. (Essendon)	182	456	2.51
Wilson, G. (Fitzroy)	268	451	1.68
Osborne, R. (Fitzroy-Sydney-Footscray)	221	482	2.18
Blight, M. (North Melbourne)	178	444	2.49
Jesaulenko, A. (Carlton-St Kilda)	279	444	1.59
Walls, R. (Carlton-Fitzroy)	259	443	1.71
Reynolds, R. (Essendon)	320	443	1.38
Dyer, J. (Richmond)	312	440	1.41
Freake, J. (Fitzroy)	174	442	2.54
Ruthven, A. (Fitzroy)	222	442	1.99
Noonan, A. (Essendon-Richmond)	192	434	2.26
Brereton, D. (Hawthorn-Sydney-Collingwood)	196	434	2.21
Richards, L. (Collingwood)	250	424	1.70
Skilton, R. (South Melbourne)	237	412	1.74
Fanning, F. (Melbourne)	104	411	3.95
Sumich, P. (West Coast)	125	453	3.62

HIGHEST GOALS AT EACH CLUB IN A CAREER

Club	Total Goals	Name	Year
Adelaide	220	Modra, Tony	1992-94
Brisbane	221	Merrett, Roger	1988-94
Carlton	722	Vallence, Harry	1926-38
Collingwood	1299	Coventry, Gordon	1920-37
Essendon	575	Madden, Simon	1974-92
Fitzroy	626	Moriarty, Jack	1924-33
Footscray	575	Beasley, Simon	1982-89
Geelong	834	Wade, Doug	1961-72
Hawthorn	1011	Dunstall, Jason	1985-94
Melbourne	546	Smith, Norm	1935-48
North Melbourne	475	Spencer, Jock	1948-57
Richmond	970	Titus, Jack	1926-43
South Melbourne	681	Pratt, Bob	1930-46
St Kilda	898	Lockett, Tony	1983-94
West Coast	453	Sumich, Peter	1989-94

HIGHEST GOALS AT EACH CLUB IN A SEASON

Club	No.	Name	Year
Hawthorn	150	Peter Hudson	1971
South Melbourne	150	Bob Pratt	1934
Collingwood	143	Peter McKenna	1970
St Kilda	132	Tony Lockett	1992
Adelaide	129	Tony Modra	1993
Geelong	129	Gary Ablett	1994
Essendon	120	John Coleman	1950
Footscray	118	Kelvin Templeton	1978
Fitzroy	116	Bernie Quinlan	1983
Carlton	115	Alex Jesaulenko	1970
Brisbane	60	Roger Merrett	1993
Richmond	112	Michael Roach	1980
West Coast	111	Peter Sumich	1991
North Melbourne	103	Doug Wade	1974
	103	Malcolm Blight	1982
Melbourne	97	Fred Fanning	1947

September's Heroes

To run out onto the Melbourne Cricket Ground on grand final day is the dream of every player. The atmosphere is electric, and the whole ground abuzz with excitement and emotion. There is an air of expectancy and uncertainty as the two opposing sides run onto the ground to be welcomed by the most famous spectator roar in Australian sport.

That good players play well in finals has long been a catchcry. It is during this time that the pressure to perform is at its greatest, and player reputations can be destroyed or enhanced by the action that takes place. The finals are also the showcase of the season, and so present some of the game's greatest moments.

Two's Better than One

The 1976 Grand Final between Hawthorn and North Melbourne was an historic one as it was the first conducted under the two-umpire system. The two men honoured with the job and who had their names placed in the record books were Bill Deller and Kevin Smith. The appointment of Smith meant he was in the record books a second time, for he was also the last man in white to single-handedly umpire a grand final, having been in charge of the 1975 match, which was also contested by Hawthorn and North.

Backman's Glory

The record books show that Melbourne's Neil 'Froggy' Crompton only kicked one goal in the 1964 season. On the surface, that is an insignificant footy fact, but put that kick and goal into the final moments of a grand final and it becomes part of football history. Collingwood, thrashed by Melbourne in the 1964 Second Semi-final, came back hard in the grand final and late in the last quarter the Magpies hit the front after a 50-metre dash by Captain Ray Gabelich gave Collingwood a goal. Collingwood looked to be home, but then Dixon of Melbourne drove the ball forward where it came off the hands of the pack to be picked up by Crompton, who had followed his rover down from the back pocket. Crompton snapped truly, and the Demons snatched the premiership from Collingwood by four points.

Seeing is Believing

The 1968 Grand Final between Carlton and Essendon was a history making game. Essendon lost captain Ken Fraser before the game, along with full-back Greg Brown, and so brought into the side a 17-year-old schoolboy, Geoff Blethyn, for his second League game at full-forward. Blethyn, wearing glasses, kicked his side's first two goals. The game see-sawed throughout, and when Blethyn took a spectacular mark and goaled in the last quarter, his fourth for the match, the Bombers trailed by one point. A point to Carlton stretched the lead by two points, then Blethyn kicked out of bounds after marking. A behind to Brent Crosswell, and the Blues were home by three points. The final score was significant: Carlton 7 goals 14 (56) points to Essendon 8 goals 5 (53) points — the first, and still the only time in history, that the losing side in a grand final kicked more goals than the winning team.

Previous page: Michael Tuck of Hawthorn and then coach Alan Joyce hold aloft the premiership cup after Hawthorn's win against West Coast in the 1991 Grand Final. (John Daniels/Sporting Pix)

How About That?

Little did we know before the bounce of the ball to start the 1979 Preliminary Final that this was going to be a game that was to change the rules of the game. Opposing each other on the ruck that day were North Melbourne's Gary Dempsey and Collingwood's Peter Moore. Gone was the art of centre bounce ruck play, as the two Brownlow medallists wrestled each other to the ground continuously throughout the game. Free kicks were scarce, as both players made it impossible for the umpire to pick who was actually doing the infringing. The situation became ludicrous, and was a blot on the game. The VFL, appalled at the prospect of ruck play becoming a wrestling match, introduced in the following year a dividing line drawn across the centre circle, separating opposing ruckmen.

Play it Again...

Only two League players have played in grand finals in successive weeks without a replay. The first was Melbourne's Stan 'Pop' Heal, who in 1941 played in Melbourne's premiership team, and then the following week turned out for West Perth who also took the flag in the WAFL competition. Heal, serving in the navy during the war years, didn't require a clearance as he was on war service. National service duty in 1969 saw Richmond's great Royce Hart play in the Tiger's premiership win over Carlton, and a week later he lined up for Glenelg against Sturt in the South Australian grand final. Hart was ko'ed early in the game, but recovered to kick three goals, and was named one of the best, while Sturt won the flag, depriving Hart of two premierships in successive weeks.

That Mark...That Kick...

The 1977 Grand Final between Collingwood and North Melbourne was the first to be telecast live throughout Victoria, and what a game it was! Well into time on, Collingwood's Ross 'Twiggy' Dunne marked a wobbly kick from teammate Billy Picken and from close in goaled to level the score. The siren sounded shortly afterwards, causing only the second grand final tie in history to be recorded. That day, Phil Baker booted six goals for the 'Roos, with Stan Alves, Wayne Schimmelbush and David Dench North's best. For the Magpies, Peter Moore kicked four goals, and their best players were Stan Magro, Len Thompson and Billy Picken.

Jock McHale, a Coaching Legend

Collingwood legend Jock McHale has a coaching record to be envied. For 38 seasons from 1912 to 1949 he led the Magpies into 17 grand finals for 8 premierships, including four in succession from 1927. McHale's one big regret would have been in 1930, when a severe attack of influenza forced him to stay in bed on doctor's orders, and he missed coaching Collingwood to a grand final victory. Another Magpie great, Bob Rush, deputised for McHale, and coached the 'Pies to a five-goal win over Geelong. Later, the excitement of Collingwood's drought-breaking premiership in 1953 proved too much for McHale, who at 71 suffered a heart attack and died several days later.

From Spoon to Flag

Fitzroy has won eight premierships since joining the League in 1897, with the last flag coming in 1944. But it was Fitzroy's win in 1916 that has to go down as one of the most unusual premiership wins in the history of the game. Due to the First World War, only four teams contested the 1916 season, and at the end of the home and away games, Fitzroy had won only two games, finishing behind Carlton with ten wins, Collingwood with six, and Richmond with five. Naturally, all four contested the finals, and Fitzroy suddenly struck form, beating Collingwood once, and Carlton twice, to take the flag.

The KO Flag

The 1973 Grand Final between Richmond and Carlton was a tough, knock-'em-down affair. The two clubs had played off for the flag the previous year, with Carlton the underdog upsetting the Tigers. The game got off to a sensational start when Tiger back-pocket player Laurie Fowler crashed into John Nicholls, the Blues captain and coach, as he juggled a mark. Nicholls goaled from the free, but the heavy blow affected his play. The second quarter was a violent one, with several fights breaking out, and Carlton's champion full-back Geoff Southby was crashed to the ground by Richmond strongman Neil Balme, and didn't appear after a long break. The Tigers led by 6 goals going into the last quarter, but a Blues fightback brought them to within 18 points of taking the lead before a goal to Balme sealed the Tigers' eighth League flag. The win capped a great day for Richmond, for earlier the club had won premierships in the Reserves, Under 19s, and Under 17s.

Opposite page: West Coast Eagle Peter Sumich shows his style in the 1992 Second Semi-final against Geelong at the MCG. (Tony Feder/Sporting Pix)

Magpie Misery

Carlton supporters will never forget Wayne Harmes, and Collingwood supporters will never forget the Blues' dynamic player. It was the last quarter of the 1979 Grand Final and Carlton led by only four points. Enter Harmes. He won the ball, and miss-kicked it downfield into the Blues' forward line. Harmes chased his kick like a man possessed, and diving at the ball hit it back into play just as it was going out of bounds. The ball landed at the feet of Blues rover Ken Sheldon, who picked up and goaled, and the Blues led by 10 points. A goal to Allan Edwards of Collingwood, and a point to Carlton rover Alex Marcou, saw the Blues hang on to win by 5 points. To this day, conjecture still rages as to whether the ball was out of bounds when Harmes knocked it back into play. The inaugural Norm Smith medal for best on the field in a grand final was awarded, and the winner was Wayne Harmes.

Hawks Home at Last

No Hawthorn supporter could ever forget 1961. The Hawks won their first AFL premiership with a relentless display of power football. Coached by the legendary John Kennedy, the Hawks, known as 'Kennedy's commandos', had won their previous twelve games before going into the 1961 Grand Final against Footscray. After trailing the Bulldogs at half-time by eight points, the Hawks produced a spirited third term, booting 6 goals 6 to Footscray's 1 goal 1, to go into the final stanza 27 points up. At the final siren, over 107 000 fans at the game acknowledged the Hawks history-making win. Champion centreman Brendan Edwards was voted best on ground with 35 kicks, and Graham Arthur had the honour of being the Hawks' first ever premiership captain.

Coach Gets it Right

Hawthorn staged a tremendous last quarter burst to take out the 1971 premiership by 7 points. Down by 20 points at three-quarter time, Hawks' coach John Kennedy swung Bob Keddie to full-forward. In a tense last term in front of 118 000 fans, Keddie booted four goals to give the Hawks their second-ever premiership. Peter Hudson that day finished with three goals for the Hawks, to take his tally to 150 goals for the season, equalling the League record held by South Melbourne great Bob Pratt.

Opposite page: Tony Shaw of Collingwood holds aloft the cup after Collingwood's much-celebrated victory over Essendon in the 1990 Grand Final. (Sporting Pix)

Sweet Success

It was called the greatest day in the short history of the Adelaide Football Club. In numerical terms, it was their 34th win since entering the AFL in 1991. The occasion: the 1993 First Elimination Final. The Crows, led by Chris McDermott, won their first ever finals match, downing Hawthorn by 15 points. Nigel Smart booted four goals for the Crows, and Tony McGuinness was voted best player. For Hawthorn, Jason Dunstall kicked six goals.

The Big Bang

The 1955 Grand Final produced one of the most bone-crunching collisions in League history. In front of 88 000 fans, Collingwood's Des Healey was racing around the outer wing of the MCG heading towards goal, thinking he was in the clear. Unbeknownst to Healey, Melbourne's 19th man Frank 'Bluey' Adams had just charged onto the ground replacing Geoff Case. Adams collided with the Magpie wingman at full throttle, leaving both men unconscious on the ground. Healey had concussion, and his nose broken in five places. Adams, who was in the play for only six seconds, woke up in hospital with a very, very sore head.

Luckless Tuck

Frank Tuck can rightly claim to be one of Collingwood's unluckiest players. In 1953, Tuck was suspended for four weeks after the last home and away game against Footscray, and missed the Magpies' premiership win. Five years later he was captain of Collingwood, but broke down at training on the eve of the 1958 Grand Final clash against Melbourne. Tuck had to agonise in the stand as his team caused the biggest upset and downed the reigning premiers. The disappointment came on top of the fact that Tuck had already played in three losing grand final teams, in 1952, 1955, and 1956.

Premiership Pain

Former Sydney coach and former Hawthorn champion Gary Buckenara will never forget his first League grand final. Picked on the half-forward flank for the Hawks against Essendon in the 1983 Grand Final, Buckenara had only one kick for the game. The statistics, of course, don't tell the full story, for in the process of kicking the ball Buckenara badly injured his knee. In front of 110 000 fans, he was carried from the field and took no further part in the Hawks' 86-point premiership win. So serious was his injury that it took until Round 22 of the following season before he again played senior football for the Hawks. Unfortunately, he was again injured and missed the finals.

The Kid's Game

Hawthorn's Dermott Brereton certainly stamped his mark on the 1985 Grand Final. In a lone hand performance against Essendon, Brereton booted 8 goals 1 from ten kicks to create at the time a new grand final goalkicking record. But even that performance wasn't good enough for the Hawks to beat the Bombers. Brereton also made news by being reported three times for striking Terry Daniher and Mark Harvey, and for crashing Paul Van Der Haar to the ground. Brereton was suspended for four weeks.

Watch your Step

Die-hard supporters of South Melbourne (now Sydney Swans) claim they should have won the 1935 premiership. South were favourites to beat Collingwood in the grand final after scoring a 21-point win over the Magpies in the Second Semi-final, but on the eve of the grand final champion full-forward Bob Pratt was knocked down by a truck on the Friday afternoon and couldn't take his place in the team. Pratt had already kicked 103 goals for the season, including six against the 'Pies in the second semi. Without Pratt's goalkicking power, South lost to Collingwood by 20 points.

The Bulldogs' First Flag

It was 1954, and Charlie Sutton, Footscray's captain and coach, led the mighty Bulldogs onto the MCG and into the history books. Built like a tank, and with his left thigh heavily strapped, Sutton was an imposing figure on the day of the grand final. For the Bulldogs it was their first ever grand final after joining the competition in 1925. For Sutton, it was an historic afternoon, and the game of his life. With full-forward Jack Collins booting seven goals, a grand final record at the time, and young Ted Whitten starring at centre half-back, and Sutton chipping in with three goals, the Bulldogs overran Melbourne to win the club's first and only ever premiership by 51 points.

Last Gasps

The lead-up finals to the 1994 Grand Final produced some of the most memorable finishes in finals history. It started with the second qualifying final, with North Melbourne playing Hawthorn at Waverley. When the siren sounded, scores were dead level: North 12 goals 19 (81), Hawthorn 13 goals 13 (81). So for the first time ever, a finals match went into extra time, with players temporarily confused about which end they had to kick to. It mattered little, for the Kangaroos blitzed the Hawks, ramming on three goals and five points to no score. That night, Footscray met Geelong in the first qualifying final match under lights at the MCG. The Cats demoralised the Bulldogs with an eight goal burst to three, with Gary Ablett booting five goals in the opening quarter. But the Bulldogs fought back to trail by 13 points at halftime, and five points at three-quarter time. When Richard Osborne goaled for Footscray with only seconds to go, Footscray looked home, but just when the champagne corks were about to explode, Bill Brownless marked for the Cats as the siren went. Brownless went back from 30 metres out with this scenario: miss everything, and Footscray wins; kick a point, and the match is a tie and into extra time; kick a goal, and the Cats are the winners and still in the finals race. Brownless simply went back and rammed the ball through the centre, and Geelong were winners by five points. In the fourth qualifying final, Collingwood played West Coast at the WACA. The 'Pies staged a great last quarter comeback to kick six goals to the Eagles' two, to get within two points after looking outclassed throughout the match. A long bomb, in the dying seconds of the last quarter, into the Collingwood forward line, saw Magpie star Mick McGuane unable to hold a mark thirty metres out from goal as the siren sounded. The game also marked the end of Tony Shaw's great career. He retired after a record of 313 games. And in the preliminary final, Geelong snatched victory after the siren yet again when Gary Ablett took a mark on the edge of the goal square. A kick from Leigh Tudor floated over the head of his opponent Mick Martyn, who had outclassed Ablett all day. With the scores level, Ablett goaled, and gave the Cats victory by six points, and a grand final shot at West Coast.

Even Stevens

The 1928 Second Semi-final between Collingwood and Melbourne produced the first tied finals match in the game's history. The Redlegs looked beaten at three-quarter time, but booted five goals straight in the last quarter with Collingwood failing to score. The match was tied up at the bell, with 9 goals 8 (62) points a piece. The replay also produced a great game. Collingwood led by only four points with only seconds to go when Melbourne rover Tom McConville missed a goal on the run, giving the 'Pies victory in the second semi. Ironically, McConville's grandson, Peter McConville, later played in Carlton's 1979 premiership team, which defeated Collingwood by five points.

Better Late than Never

Melbourne great Robert Flower had to wait until the end of his illustrious career before playing in a finals game. The Demons in 1987 made a late charge, and grabbed fifth spot and a piece of September action. Flower led his team into three finals before losing the preliminary final to Hawthorn by two points. Those games were to be his last of his 274 games career. Flower holds one unique finals records, in that no player had played as many games — 271 — before making his finals debut.

The Umpire Quits

Fortunately for field umpire Alan Coward, the 1939 Grand Final was a one-sided affair with Melbourne thrashing Collingwood by 53 points. But Coward in the second term tripped over in a thick of players and dislocated his elbow. Play continued for a short time with Coward on the ground suffering extreme pain. Melbourne kicked a goal during the umpiring crisis, but it was disallowed because Coward could not give the all clear. Coward had to leave the field and was replaced by emergency umpire Bill Blackburn.

Blue Legends

The 1993 finals series saw the first AFL final played under lights, when Carlton and Essendon clashed at the MCG in the qualifying final; 79 739 fans turned up to the historic match and saw Carlton snatch victory by two points. Blues captain Stephen 'Sticks' Kernahan starred with six goals, and in doing so became only the second Carlton player ever to reach 500 career goals. Former great Harry 'Soapy' Vallence, with 722 goals, heads the Blues list.

Any Witnesses?

The 1965 Preliminary Final between Collingwood and Essendon is famous for two reasons: firstly, it was in this game that Collingwood introduced a beanstalk young ruckman named Len Thompson for his first senior game. 'Thommo' went on to become one of the all-time greats, playing over 300 games and winning the 1972 Brownlow medal. And secondly, it is famous for the John Somerville incident. Just after half-time, Essendon's Somerville was sprawled out on the ground unconscious, and no-one in the crowd of 95 000 saw what happened. The nearest Collingwood player to him was defender Duncan Wright. From that moment on, Wright was booed every time he went near the ball. Somerville spent several days in hospital and wasn't fit to play the following week in Essendon's premiership win. Speaking on the incident many years later, Wright did not admit he was responsible for the knock-out blow. He said, 'That's something I might tell on my deathbed.'

The Finals System

In the past, many different systems have been used to determine the premiership team. Between 1897 and 1902, the eight teams in the competition played each other twice and then the top four teams played off in a round-robin series to decide the premiers. From 1902 to 1924 the teams were split into two divisions with the winners of the respective divisions meeting in the grand final. In 1924, the round-robin series was revised and the team with the best percentage was awarded the premiership. From 1925 to 1930 the top four teams played off for the premiership; first played third and second played fourth with the winners playing off in the grand final.

The McIntyre Final Four was introduced in 1931. It consisted of a first and second semi-final, a preliminary Final and the grand final. Third and fourth played in the first semi-final — the loser was eliminated and the winner advanced to the preliminary final. First and second played in the second semi-final — the winner advanced to the grand final and the loser to the preliminary final. The winner of the preliminary final advanced to the grand final and the loser was eliminated.

The McIntyre system was a great success and no changes were made for more than forty years. Then in 1972 it was adapted to accommodate a Final Five, including an elimination final and a qualifying final. The competition expanded with the addition of non-Victorian teams and a second elimination final was added for the Final Six in 1991. When the Final Eight was introduced in 1994, three more qualifying finals were added, creating the finals series that we have today with up to nine matches played over four weeks.

• Quick Quiz •

1   In which season was the Final Five introduced into League football?

2   Which League club made its first finals appearance in 1957?

3   At which venue was the 1945 finals series played?

4   Which League player holds the record for playing in the most matches without a finals appearance?

5   How many Hawthorn premiership teams included Michael Tuck?

6   Name the Hawthorn players who have won the Norm Smith medal for best on the ground in a grand final.

7   Name the player who has played the most games in finals, and how many.

8   Name the only player from the 1977 drawn grand final between Collingwood and North Melbourne not to play in the replay grand final.

9   In reference to question 8, who was this player's replacement?

10 Name the player who has played in the most League grand finals without winning a premiership.

GRAND FINAL SCORES AND ATTENDANCES

Season	Clubs and Final Score	Attendance
1897*	**Essendon** — v Geelong	—
1898	**Fitzroy 5.8** v Essendon 3.5	16 000
1899	**Fitzroy 3.9** v South Melbourne 3.8	4000
1900	**Melbourne 4.10** v Fitzroy 3.12	20 000
1901	**Essendon 6.7** v Collingwood 2.4	30 000
1902	**Collingwood 9.6** v Essendon 3.9	35 000
1903	**Collingwood 4.7** v Fitzroy 3.11	32 363
1904	**Fitzroy 9.7** v Carlton 5.7	32 688
1905	**Fitzroy 4.6** v Collingwood 2.5	30 000
1906	**Carlton 15.4** v Fitzroy 6.9	44 437
1907	**Carlton 6.14** v South Melbourne 6.9	40 485
1908	**Carlton 5.5** v Essendon 3.8	50 261
1909	**South Melbourne 4.14** v Carlton 4.12	36 700
1910	**Collingwood 9.7** v Carlton 6.11	43 000
1911	**Essendon 5.11** v Collingwood 4.11	44 000
1912	**Essendon 5.17** v South Melbourne 4.9	54 463
1913	**Fitzroy 7.14** v St Kilda 5.13	59 479
1914	**Carlton 6.9** v South Melbourne 4.15	30 427
1915	**Carlton 11.12** v Collingwood 6.9	39 211
1916	**Fitzroy 12.13** v Carlton 8.8	20 953
1917	**Collingwood 9.20** v Fitzroy 5.9	28 385
1918	**South Melbourne 9.8** v Collingwood 7.15	39 168
1919	**Collingwood 11.12** v Richmond 7.11	47 000
1920	**Richmond 7.10** v Collingwood 5.5	53 908
1921	**Richmond 5.6** v Carlton 4.8	43 122
1922	**Fitzroy 11.13** v Collingwood 9.14	50 054
1923	**Essendon 8.15** v Fitzroy 6.10	46 566
1924*	**Essendon** — v Richmond	—
1925	**Geelong 10.19** v Collingwood 9.15	64 288
1926	**Melbourne 17.17** v Collingwood 9.8	59 362
1927	**Collingwood 2.13** v Richmond 1.7	34 551
1928	**Collingwood 13.18** v Richmond 9.9	50 026
1929	**Collingwood 11.13** v Richmond 7.8	63 336
1930	**Collingwood 14.16** v Geelong 9.16	45 022
1931	**Geelong 9.14** v Richmond 7.6	60 712
1932	**Richmond 13.14** v Carlton 12.11	69 724
1933	**South Melbourne 9.17** v Richmond 4.5	75 754
1934	**Richmond 19.14** v South Melbourne 12.17	65 335
1935	**Collingwood 11.12** v South Melbourne 7.16	54 154
1936	**Collingwood 11.23** v South Melbourne 10.18	74 091
1937	**Geelong 18.14** v Collingwood 12.18	88 540
1938	**Carlton 15.10** v Collingwood 13.7	96 834
1939	**Melbourne 21.22** v Collingwood 14.11	78 110
1940	**Melbourne 15.17** v Richmond 10.8	69 061
1941	**Melbourne 19.13** v Essendon 13.20	79 687

GRAND FINAL SCORES AND ATTENDANCES (cont.)

1942	**Essendon 19.18** v Richmond 11.13	49 000
1943	**Richmond 12.14** v Essendon 11.15	42 100
1944	**Fitzroy 9.12** v Richmond 7.9	43 000
1945	**Carlton 15.13** v South Melbourne 10.15	62 986
1946	**Essendon 22.18** v Melbourne 13.9	73 743
1947	**Carlton 13.8** v Essendon 11.19	85 815
1948	**Melbourne 13.11** v Essendon 7.8	85 658
1949	**Essendon 18.17** v Carlton 6.16	90 453
1950	**Essendon 13.14** v North Melbourne 7.12	87 601
1951	**Geelong 11.15** v Essendon 10.10	85 795
1952	**Geelong 13.8** v Collingwood 5.10	82 890
1953	**Collingwood 11.11** v Geelong 8.17	89 060
1954	**Footscray 15.12** v Melbourne 7.9	80 897
1955	**Melbourne 8.16** v Collingwood 5.6	88 053
1956	**Melbourne 17.19** v Collingwood 6.12	115 802
1957	**Melbourne 17.14** v Essendon 7.13	100 324
1958	**Collingwood 12.10** v Melbourne 9.10	97 956
1959	**Melbourne 17.13** v Essendon 11.12	103 506
1960	**Melbourne 8.14** v Collingwood 2.2	97 457
1961	**Hawthorn 13.16** v Footscray 7.9	107 935
1962	**Essendon 13.12** v Carlton 8.10	98 385
1963	**Geelong 15.19** v Hawthorn 8.12	101 209
1964	**Melbourne 8.16** v Collingwood 8.12	102 469
1965	**Essendon 14.21** v St Kilda 9.16	104 846
1966	**St Kilda 10.14** v Collingwood 10.13	101 655
1967	**Richmond 16.18** v Geelong 15.15	109 396
1968	**Carlton 7.14** v Essendon 8.5	116 828
1969	**Richmond 12.13** v Carlton 8.12	119 165
1970	**Carlton 17.9** v Collingwood 14.17	121 696
1971	**Hawthorn 12.10** v St Kilda 11.9	118 192
1972	**Carlton 28.9** v Richmond 22.18	112 393
1973	**Richmond 16.20** v Carlton 12.14	116 956
1974	**Richmond 18.20** v North Melbourne 13.9	113 839
1975	**North Melbourne 19.8** v Hawthorn 9.13	110 551
1976	**Hawthorn 13.22** v North Melbourne 10.10	110 143
1977	**North Melbourne 21.25** v Collingwood 19.10	95 366
1978	**Hawthorn 18.13** v North Melbourne 15.13	101 704
1979	**Carlton 11.16** v Collingwood 11.11	112 845
1980	**Richmond 23.21** v Collingwood 9.24	113 461
1981	**Carlton 12.20** v Collingwood 10.12	115 964
1982	**Carlton 14.19** v Richmond 12.13	107 536
1983	**Hawthorn 20.20** v Essendon 8.9	110 332
1984	**Essendon 14.21** v Hawthorn 12.9	92 685
1985	**Essendon 26.14** v Hawthorn 14.8	100 042
1986	**Hawthorn 16.14** v Carlton 9.14	101 861
1987	**Carlton 15.14** v Hawthorn 9.17	92 754
1988	**Hawthorn 22.20** v Melbourne 6.20	93 754

GRAND FINAL SCORES AND ATTENDANCES (cont.)

1989	**Hawthorn 21.18** v Geelong 21.12	94 796
1990	**Collingwood 13.11** v Essendon 5.11	98 944
1991	**Hawthorn 20.19** v West Coast 13.8	75 230
1992	**West Coast 16.17** v Geelong 12.11	95 007
1993	**Essendon 20.13** v Carlton 13.11	96 862
1994	**West Coast 20.23** v Geelong 8.15	93 860

* No Grand Final

FINAL BY FINAL STATISTICS

Elimination Final 1972–1994
Highest score:
St Kilda 24.14 (158) v Essendon 13.13 (91), 1973.
Melbourne 22.16 (158) v North Melbourne 5.10 (40), 1987.

Lowest score:
North Melbourne 5.10 (40) v Melbourne 22.16 (158), 1987.

Highest winning margin:
118 points - Melbourne 22.16 (158) v North Melbourne 5.10 (40), 1987.

Lowest winning margin:
1 point - Fitzroy 8.10 (58) v Essendon 8.9. (57), 1986.

Highest aggregate:
260 points - Collingwood 23.15 (153) v Fitzroy 15.17 (107).

Highest attendance:
82 952 - North Melbourne v Collingwood (1980).

Lowest attendance:
29 147 - North Melbourne v West Coast (1993).

Best goalscorers:
9 - T. Lockett (St Kilda), 1991. 8 - B. Brownless (Geelong), 1991.

Qualifying Final 1972–1994
Highest score:
Geelong 26.16 (172) v Footscray 17.9 (111), 1992.

Lowest score:
Sydney 8.9 (57) v Hawthorn 23.18 (156), 1987.

Lowest winning margin:
2 points - West Coast 11.16 (82) v Collingwood 12.8 (80), 1994.

Highest winning margin:
99 points - Hawthorn 23.18 (156) v Sydney 8.9 (57), 1987.

Highest aggregate:
284 points - Richmond 25.14 (164) v Collingwood 18.12 (120), 1972.

FINAL BY FINAL STATISTICS (cont.)

Highest attendance:
91 900 - Richmond v Collingwood, 1972.

Lowest attendance:
31 824 - West Coast v Collingwood, 1994.

Drawn game:
Collingwood 13.12 (80) v West Coast 13.12 (80) 1990. Collingwood won the play-off 19.12 (126) to 9.13 (67).

Best goalscorers:
9 - B. Brownless (Geelong), 1992. 8 - W. Ralph (Carlton), 1984; M. Moncrieff (Hawthorn), 1978; B. Quinlan (Fitzroy), 1983.

First Semi-Final 1931–1994
Highest score:
Richmond 25.17 (167) v Geelong 7.7 (49), 1969.

Lowest score:
Essendon 5.11 (41) v Footscray 6.13 (49), 1953.

Highest winning margin:
118 points - Richmond 25.17 (167) v Geelong 7.7 (49), 1969.

Lowest winning margin:
1 point - Collingwood 19.19 (133) v Fitzroy 19.18 (132), 1981.

Highest aggregate:
280 points - Hawthorn 24.22 (166) v North Melbourne 18.6 (114), 1982.

Highest attendance:
104 239 - St Kilda v South Melbourne, 1970.

Lowest attendance:
41 136 - West Coast v Melbourne, 1991.

Best goalscorers:
11 - H. Vallence (Carlton), 1931. 8 - L. Collins (Carlton), 1945; W. Twomey (Collingwood), 1948; D. Wade (Geelong), 1967.

Second Semi-Final 1931–1994
Highest score:
Geelong 22.20 (152) v Collingwood 10.10 (70), 1951.

Lowest score:
Collingwood 4.9 (33) v Melbourne 11.12 (78), 1958.

Highest winning margin:
89 points - Melbourne 19.20 (134) v Collingwood 6.9 (45), 1964.

FINAL BY FINAL STATISTICS (cont.)

Lowest winning margin:
1 point - St Kilda 13.24 (102) v Collingwood 14.17 (101), 1965.

Highest aggregate:
242 points - Richmond 20.21 (141) v Carlton 14.17 (101), 1967.

Highest attendance:
112 838 - Collingwood v Carlton, 1970.

Lowest attendance:
35 934 - Richmond v Geelong, 1934.

Drawn games:
Essendon 14.16 (100) v Collingwood 13.22 (100), 1946. Essendon won the play-off. Carlton 8.13 (55) v Richmond, 1972. Richmond won the play-off.

Postponements:
August 24, 1918, because of rain. South Melbourne 8.10 (58) defeated Carlton 7.11 (53) the following week.

Best goalscorers:
11 - G. Goninon (Geelong), 1951. 9 - P. McKenna (Collingwood), 1970. 8 - J. Metherell (Geelong), 1937; K. Baxter (Carlton), 1938; A. Jesaulenko (Carlton), 1970; K. Bartlett (Richmond), 1980; P. Sumich (West Coast), 1992.

Preliminary Final 1931–1994
Highest score:
Essendon 28.6 (174) v Collingwood 5.11 (41), 1984.

Lowest score:
Footscray 5.7 (37) v Geelong 8.15 (63), 1953.

Highest winning margin:
133 points - Essendon 28.6 (174) v Collingwood 5.11 (41), 1984.

Lowest winning margin:
1 point - North Melbourne 10.7 (67) v Carlton 9.12 (66). 2 points - Essendon 10.10 (70) v Collingwood 10.8 (68), 1951; Hawthorn 11.14 (80) v Melbourne 10.18 (78).

Highest aggregate:
242 points - Essendon 25.14 (164) v North Melbourne 12.6 (78), 1983.

Highest attendance:
108 215 - Carlton v St Kilda, 1970.

Lowest attendance:
1934, when only 34 000 saw the match because of bad weather.

Drawn games:
Carlton 12.13 (85) v Geelong 13.7 (85) in 1962. Carlton won the play-off.

FINAL BY FINAL STATISTICS (cont.)

Best goalscorers:
11 - H. Vallence (Carlton), 1932; R. Todd (Collingwood), 1938, 1939. 9 - L. White (South Melbourne), 1942; J. Dyer (Richmond), 1944.

Grand Final 1931–1994
Highest score:
Carlton 28.9 (177) v Richmond, 1972.

Lowest score:
Collingwood 2.2 (14) v Melbourne, 1960.

Highest aggregate:
327 points - Carlton 28.9 (177) v Richmond 22.18 (150), 1972.

Greatest winning margin:
96 points - Hawthorn 22.20 (152) v Melbourne 6.20 (56), 1988.

Lowest winning margin:
1 point - Carlton 13.8 (86) v Essendon 11.19 (85), 1947; St Kilda 10.14 (74) v Collingwood 10.13 (73), 1966.

Drawn games:
Essendon 7.27 (69) v Melbourne 10.9 (69), 1948; Collingwood 10.16 (76) v North Melbourne 9.22 (76), 1977.

Highest attendance:
121 696 - Carlton v Collingwood, 1970.

Lowest attendance:
42 100 in 1943.

Postponements:
The 1923 match was postponed one week because the MCG was waterlogged. Essendon 8.15 (63) defeated Fitzroy 6.10 (46) the following week.

Best goalscorers:
9 - G. Ablett (Geelong), 1989. 8 - D. Brereton (Hawthorn), 1985. 7 - N. Smith (Melbourne), 1940; R. Harris (Richmond), 1943; T. Reynolds (Essendon), 1943; G. Lane (Essendon), 1946; J. Collins (Footscray), 1954; E. Fordham (Essendon), 1965; A. Jesaulenko (Carlton), 1972; K. Bartlett (Richmond), 1980.

NUMBER OF PREMIERSHIPS PER CLUB 1897–1994

Collingwood	14	Hawthorn	9
Carlton	15	St Kilda	1
Essendon	15	North Melbourne	2
Geelong	6	Footscray	1
Richmond	10	West Coast	2
Melbourne	12	Adelaide	–
Fitzroy	8	Brisbane	–
South Melb/Sydney	3		

MOST FINALS MATCHES 1897–1994

39 — M. Tuck (Hawthorn)
31 — G. Coventry (Collingwood)
29 — W. Schimmelbusch (North Melbourne)
   L. Matthews (Hawthorn)
   B. Doull (Carlton)
28 — W. Hutchison (Essendon)
   C. Mew (Hawthorn)
   G. Ayres (Hawthorn)
27 — H. Collier (Collingwood)
   R. Reynolds (Essendon)
   K. Bartlett (Richmond)

MOST PREMIERSHIPS 1897–1994

7 — M. Tuck (Hawthorn)
6 — A. Collier (Collingwood)
   H. Collier (Collingwood)
   F. Adams (Melbourne)
   R. Barassi (Melbourne)

MOST GRAND FINALS 1897–1994

11 — M. Tuck (Hawthorn)
10 — G. Coventry (Collingwood)
   A. Collier (Collingwood)
   W. Hutchison (Essendon)
   R. Reynolds (Essendon)

NORM SMITH MEDALLISTS

Norm Smith was a famous Melbourne full-forward and coach. He was also associated with Fitzroy and South Melbourne. He played a total of 227 games and coached 452, including six grand finals for Melbourne in the '50s and '60s. He died in 1973, aged 57.

1979 — W. Harmes (Carlton)
1980 — K. Bartlett (Richmond)
1981 — B. Doull (Carlton)
1982 — M. Rioli (Richmond)
1983 — C. Robertson (Hawthorn)
1984 — B. Duckworth (Essendon)
1985 — S. Madden (Essendon)
1986 — G. Ayres (Hawthorn)

1987 — D. Rhys-Jones (Carlton)
1988 — G. Ayres (Hawthorn)
1989 — G. Ablett (Geelong)
1990 — A. Shaw (Collingwood)
1991 — P. Dear (Hawthorn)
1992 — P. Matera (West Coast)
1993 — M. Long (Essendon)
1994 — D. Kemp (West Coast)

FINALS MAKE-UP

Season	First	Second	Third	Fourth	Fifth	Sixth
1897*	Essendon	Geelong	Collingwood	Melbourne		
1898	Fitzroy	Essendon	Collingwood	Geelong		
1899	Fitzroy	Sth Melbourne	Geelong	Collingwood		
1900	Melbourne	Fitzroy	Essendon	Collingwood		
1901	Essendon	Collingwood	Geelong	Fitzroy		
1902	Collingwood	Essendon	Fitzroy	Melbourne		
1903	Collingwood	Fitzroy	Carlton	Geelong		
1904	Fitzroy	Carlton	Collingwood	Essendon		
1905	Fitzroy	Collingwood	Carlton	Essendon		
1906	Carlton	Fitzroy	Collingwood	Essendon		
1907	Carlton	Sth Melbourne	St Kilda	Collingwood		
1908	Carlton	Essendon	St Kilda	Collingwood		
1909	Sth Melbourne	Carlton	Collingwood	Essendon		
1910	Collingwood	Carlton	Sth Melbourne	Essendon		
1911	Essendon	Collingwood	Sth Melbourne	Carlton		
1912	Essendon	Sth Melbourne	Carlton	Geelong		
1913	Fitzroy	St Kilda	Sth Melbourne	Collingwood		
1914	Carlton	Sth Melbourne	Fitzroy	Geelong		
1915	Carlton	Collingwood	Fitzroy	Melbourne		
1916	Fitzroy	Carlton	Collingwood	Richmond		
1917	Collingwood	Fitzroy	Carlton	Sth Melbourne		
1918	Sth Melbourne	Collingwood	Carlton	St Kilda		
1919	Collingwood	Richmond	Sth Melbourne	Carlton		
1920	Richmond	Collingwood	Carlton	Fitzroy		
1921	Richmond	Carlton	Collingwood	Geelong		
1922	Fitzroy	Collingwood	Essendon	Carlton		
1923	Essendon	Fitzroy	Sth Melbourne	Geelong		
1924*	Essendon	Richmond	Fitzroy	Sth Melbourne		
1925	Geelong	Collingwood	Melbourne	Essendon		
1926	Melbourne	Collingwood	Essendon	Geelong		

FINALS MAKE-UP (cont.)

Season	First	Second	Third	Fourth	Fifth	Sixth
1927	Collingwood	Richmond	Geelong	Carlton		
1928	Collingwood	Richmond	Melbourne	Carlton		
1929	Collingwood	Richmond	Carlton	St Kilda		
1930	Collingwood	Geelong	Carlton	Richmond		
1931	Geelong	Richmond	Carlton	Collingwood		
1932	Richmond	Carlton	Collingwood	Sth Melbourne		
1933	Sth Melbourne	Richmond	Geelong	Carlton		
1934	Richmond	Sth Melbourne	Geelong	Collingwood		
1935	Collingwood	Sth Melbourne	Richmond	Carlton		
1936	Collingwood	Sth Melbourne	Melbourne	Carlton		
1937	Geelong	Collingwood	Melbourne	Richmond		
1938	Carlton	Collingwood	Geelong	Footscray		
1939	Melbourne	Collingwood	St Kilda	Richmond		
1940	Melbourne	Richmond	Essendon	Geelong		
1941	Melbourne	Essendon	Carlton	Richmond		
1942	Essendon	Richmond	Sth Melbourne	Footscray		
1943	Richmond	Essendon	Fitzroy	Carlton		
1944	Fitzroy	Richmond	Essendon	Footscray		
1945	Carlton	Sth Melbourne	Collingwood	Nth Melbourne		
1946	Essendon	Melbourne	Collingwood	Footscray		
1947	Carlton	Essendon	Fitzroy	Richmond		
1948	Melbourne	Essendon	Collingwood	Footscray		
1949	Essendon	Carlton	Nth Melbourne	Collingwood		
1950	Essendon	Nth Melbourne	Geelong	Melbourne		
1951	Geelong	Essendon	Collingwood	Footscray		
1952	Geelong	Collingwood	Fitzroy	Carlton		
1953	Collingwood	Geelong	Footscray	Essendon		
1954	Footscray	Melbourne	Geelong	Nth Melbourne		
1955	Melbourne	Collingwood	Geelong	Essendon		
1956	Melbourne	Collingwood	Footscray	Geelong		
1957	Melbourne	Essendon	Hawthorn	Carlton		
1958	Collingwood	Melbourne	Nth Melbourne	Fitzroy		
1959	Melbourne	Essendon	Carlton	Collingwood		
1960	Melbourne	Collingwood	Fitzroy	Essendon		
1961	Hawthorn	Footscray	Melbourne	St Kilda		
1962	Essendon	Carlton	Geelong	Melbourne		
1963	Geelong	Hawthorn	Melbourne	St Kilda		
1964	Melbourne	Collingwood	Geelong	Essendon		
1965	Essendon	St Kilda	Collingwood	Geelong		
1966	St Kilda	Collingwood	Essendon	Geelong		
1967	Richmond	Geelong	Carlton	Collingwood		
1968	Carlton	Essendon	Geelong	St Kilda		
1969	Richmond	Carlton	Collingwood	Geelong		
1970	Carlton	Collingwood	St Kilda	Sth Melbourne		
1971	Hawthorn	St Kilda	Richmond	Collingwood		

FINALS MAKE-UP (cont.)

Season	First	Second	Third	Fourth	Fifth	Sixth
1972	Carlton	Richmond	St Kilda	Collingwood	Essendon	
1973	Richmond	Carlton	Collingwood	St Kilda	Essendon	
1974	Richmond	Nth Melbourne	Hawthorn	Collingwood	Footscray	
1975	Nth Melbourne	Hawthorn	Richmond	Carlton	Collingwood	
1976	Hawthorn	Nth Melbourne	Carlton	Geelong	Footscray	
1977	Nth Melbourne	Collingwood	Hawthorn	Richmond	Sth Melbourne	
1978	Hawthorn	Nth Melbourne	Collingwood	Carlton	Geelong	
1979	Carlton	Collingwood	Nth Melbourne	Fitzroy	Essendon	
1980	Richmond	Collingwood	Geelong	Carlton	Nth Melbourne	
1981	Carlton	Collingwood	Geelong	Fitzroy	Essendon	
1982	Carlton	Richmond	Hawthorn	Nth Melbourne	Essendon	
1983	Hawthorn	Essendon	Nth Melbourne	Fitzroy	Carlton	
1984	Essendon	Hawthorn	Collingwood	Carlton	Fitzroy	
1985	Essendon	Hawthorn	Footscray	Nth Melbourne	Carlton	
1986	Hawthorn	Carlton	Fitzroy	Sydney	Essendon	
1987	Carlton	Hawthorn	Melbourne	Sydney	Nth Melbourne	
1988	Hawthorn	Melbourne	Carlton	Collingwood	West Coast	
1989	Hawthorn	Geelong	Essendon	Melbourne	Collingwood	
1990	Collingwood	Essendon	West Coast	Melbourne	Hawthorn	
1991	Hawthorn	West Coast	Geelong	Melbourne	St Kilda	Essendon
1992	West Coast	Geelong	Footscray	St Kilda	Collingwood	Hawthorn
1993	Essendon	Carlton	Adelaide	West Coast	Nth Melbourne	Hawthorn
1994	West Coast	Geelong	Nth Melbourne	Melbourne	Carlton	Footscray

*No Grand Final
In 1897 and 1924 the premiership was won by the team which performed best in its three finals matches.

Aye, Aye, Skipper!

Captains come in all shapes and sizes, and with all kinds of personalities. There have been the famous skippers who have led by their physical presence and their follow-me, knock-'em-down attitude. Then there are others who have inspired teammates in a much quieter way with sheer skill that captures the imagination and respect of their peers.

Being appointed captain is one of the greatest honours a club can bestow upon a player. It's the recognition of the captain's leadership qualities, and his ability to lead the troops onto the field of battle, and to be the on-field extension of the coach.

There is much more to being a good captain than just tossing the coin at the start of the game!

Three League captains have played Test cricket for Australia. Essendon's Dave Smith lead the Bombers in 23 games including its 1911 premiership win, and played two Tests in England in 1912, scoring 30 runs at an average of 15.

• • •

Roy Park captained University on two occasions in 1914. He made one Test appearance in the 1920-21 season against England at the MCG. Park didn't trouble the scorer for he was bowled first ball for a golden duck in Australia's only innings. Park bowled one over for nine runs.

• • •

South Melbourne star Laurie Nash is regarded as one of the greatest football-ers of all time. During the 1937 League season he led South in 13 games. Nash, without playing Shield cricket, was selected to play Test cricket for Australia against South Africa at the MCG in 1932. He destroyed the Spring-boks, taking 4 for 18 from twelve overs in their first innings, and 1 for 64 off seven overs in the second innings. It was another five years before Nash again played Test cricket. This time it was against England in the fifth Test of 1937 at the MCG. Nash again was spectacular, taking 4 for 70 and 1 for 34 in Australia's victory by an innings.

• • •

The world's most famous professional footrace, the Stawell Gift, has been won by four League captains: Essendon's George Stuckey, who led the Bombers in 60 games, won the Gift in 1897; Norman Clark took out the famous race in 1899. He later captained Carlton on six occasions in 1907. Bill Twomey snr played with Collingwood and Hawthorn, and won Stawell in 1924. Twomey skippered Hawthorn nine times in 1933. His three sons, Bill, Mick and Pat, all played in Collingwood's 1953 Premiership side. And Jack Grant captained Geelong in ten games between 1945 and 1946. He won the great race in 1938.

• • •

In 1905, St.Kilda recruited J. Wearmouth. Wearmouth made his debut against Essendon and played a fine game. Through injury, he missed the next game, but was selected the following week for the Carlton clash. The Saints lost their captain Vic Barwick and vice-captain Bill 'Win' Outen through injury, and surprisingly named Wearmouth as skipper for the game. St Kilda went down to Carlton and Wearmouth never played League football again.

• • •

North Melbourne fullback and premiership star David Dench is the youngest player to captain a League club. Dench was 20 years and 222 days of age when he led the Kangaroos against St Kilda at Moorabbin in Round 1 of 1972. The second youngest-ever captain is again a North Melbourne player. Wayne Carey was 21 years 304 days when he skippered North for the first time against Brisbane at the MCG in Round 1, 1993.

• • •

Thirty League players have played 300 games or more in League matches. Only three members of the 300 club never captained their club's side on any occasion. They are: Bruce Doull, Carlton, 359 games; Russell Greene, St Kilda and Hawthorn, 304 games; and Gary Foulds, Essendon, 300 games. Ironically, Greene captained Victoria against Western Australia in 1985.

• • •

The oldest players to captain a League side are Ted Rankin, Geelong, 1909; Sid Barker, North Melbourne, 1927; Michael Tuck for Hawthorn in 1991. All three had turned 37 before leading their clubs for the last time.

• • •

Fitzroy great Kevin Murray had a frustrating time as captain of the Lions. Murray was skipper for 158 matches between 1963 and 1972, but never led his team in a finals match. He also was captain and coach of Fitzroy for two seasons, without leading his team to victory. The Lions won only one game under his coaching, but Murray missed the game for he was representing Victoria in state football when his beloved Lions upset Geelong in 1963. Wally Clark was Fitzroy's acting coach that day. Other long-serving captains never to lead their teams into finals are South Melbourne's Ron Clegg, 106 games, and Richmond's Des Rowe, 103 games.

• • •

Essendon's Dick Reynold's holds the League record for captaining his club in the most matches. Reynold's led the Bombers in 224 of his 320 career appearances. Footscray's Ted Whitten is next best with 212 games as captain of the Bulldogs in his 321-game career.

Opposite page: Carlton Captain Stephen Kernahan
(Robert Banks/Sporting Pix)

• • •

South Melbourne holds the record for the most captains in a season. In 1937, five players had the honour: Laurie Nash, the official skipper, was injured, and in remaining games was replaced by Austin Robertson snr, Maurie 'Mocha' Johnson, Terry Brain, and Bill Faul.

• • •

Fitzroy ruckman Frank Curcio first led the 'Roys as acting captain in 1934 against St Kilda at the Junction Oval. In 1938, he was appointed club captain, a position he held until 1941. In 1948 he again tossed the coin as acting skipper, ironically against St Kilda, at the Junction Oval. In doing so, Curcio created a League record of 13 years 335 days from first match as captain to last match as skipper.

• • •

It's unusual to see both club captain and vice-captain playing in the Reserves. It last happened in Rounds 9 and 10 during the 1994 season, when Footscray's leaders Scott Wynd and Simon Atkins lined up in the Twos. Such a situation has happened at least on two other occasions, the first time in 1954 when North Melbourne's on-field leaders Gerald Marchesi and Jack O'Halloran played in the seconds after returning from injury. And in 1962, in the last home and away game, Geelong skipper John Yeates and his deputy John Devine, both lined up in the Seconds against Fitzroy. Both players were also returning from injury.

• • •

In League football, there are only four occasions on record where opposing captains have been brothers. It first occurred in Round 5 in 1900 when Essendon's George Stuckey tossed the coin with his brother Bill who played for Carlton. George was the successful captain that day. In 1912, opposing brothers again led the teams into battle. The occasion was the first semi-final between Essendon and South Melbourne at the MCG. Alan Belcher was captain of the 'Dons with brother Vic leading South. Essendon and Alan won the day. On 7 July 1928, the Scanlan brothers, Joe and Paddy, faced each other as captains when Footscray played South Melbourne at the Western Oval. Bulldog Joe took the points. And in 1989, in a pre-season night game, Gerard Healy led Sydney against brother Greg (Melbourne) at Waverley Park. Greg was laughing after the game.

• • •

There have been eight cases of fathers and sons captaining League teams:

Fathers	Sons
Charlie Pannam snr (Collingwood)	Charlie (Collingwood) Alby (Collingwood)
Ted Rankin (Geelong)	Bert Rankin (Geelong) Cliff Rankin (Geelong)
Bill Thomas (South Melbourne)	Len Thomas (South Melbourne, Hawthorn, North Melbourne)
Harry Cordner (University)	Don Cordner (Melbourne) Dennis Cordner (Melbourne)
Bob Nash (Collingwood)	Laurie Nash (South Melbourne)
Geoff Moriarty (Fitzroy)	Jack Moriarty (Fitzroy)
Bill Twomey snr (Hawthorn)	Bill Twomey jnr (Collingwood)
Arthur Stevens (Footscray)	Harvey Stevens (Footscray)

• • •

The most successful captains in leading sides to premierships are Essendon's Dick Reynolds, who led the Bombers into nine grand finals for four wins, and Sid Coventry of Collingwood, who captained the Magpies to four successive flags in 1927 through to 1930.

• • •

Triple Brownlow medallist Bob Skilton, despite missing all the 1969 season due to an Achilles tendon operation, held the captaincy of South Melbourne from 1961 until his retirement at the end of the 1971 season. Richmond's Dan Minogue led the Tigers from 1920 until 1925, captaining the side in 94 of its 95 matches. Minogue missed Round 17 in 1920 through injury.

• • •

At least nine pairs of brothers have captained the same League club:

*   Harry and Ted Cordner, University, 16 games
*   Bert and Cliff Rankin, Geelong, 79 games
*   Alby and Charlie Pannam jnr, Collingwood, 25 games
*   Sid and Gordon Coventry, Collingwood, 155 games
*   Albert and Harry Collier, Collingwood, 99 games
*   Don and Dennis Cordner, Melbourne, 97 games
*   Wayne and Max Richardson, Collingwood, 141 games
*   Ian and Bruce Nankervis, Geelong, 140 games
*   Ray and Tony Shaw, Collingwood, 188 games.

• • •

Since 1933, eight League captains have kicked ten goals or more in a match:

1933:   Jack Moriarty, Fitzroy
        10 goals against Collingwood at the Brunswick Street Oval.
1948:   Jack Graham, South Melbourne
        10 goals against Geelong at Kardinia Park.
1948:   Lindsay White, Geelong
        11 goals against St. Kilda at Kardinia Park.
1950:   Lindsay White, Geelong
        10 goals against Hawthorn at Glenferrie Oval.
1972:   Doug Wade, Geelong
        11 goals against Richmond at the MCG.
1976:   Robert Walls, Carlton
        10 goals against. Richmond at Princes Park.
1981:   Leigh Matthews, Hawthorn
        11 goals against Melbourne at the MCG.
1983:   Bernie Quinlan, Fitzroy,
        10 goals against St Kilda at Moorabbin.
1989:   Stephen Kernahan, Carlton
        10 goals against Richmond at Princes Park.
1994:   Garry Lyon, Melbourne
        10 goals against Footscray at the MCG.

• • •

In the history of the Brownlow medal, only 11 captains have won the covetted award. Ivor Warne Smith, Melbourne, in 1928; Allan Hopkins, Footscray, in

1930; Herbie Matthews, South Melbourne, in 1940; Norman Ware, Footscray, in 1941; Alan Ruthven, Fitzroy, in 1950; Bill Hutchison, Essendon, in 1952 and 1953; Neil Roberts, St. Kilda, 1958; Bob Skilton, South Melbourne, 1963 and 1968; Kevin Murray, Fitzroy, 1969; Graham Moss, Essendon, 1976; and Barry Round, South Melbourne, in 1981.

• • •

Only three players in the history of the game have captained as many as three League clubs. Dan Minogue, George Heinz, and Len Thomas share this unique record. Minogue captained Collingwood in 41 games between 1914 and 1916; he then led Richmond for 94 matches from 1920 to 1925, including back-to-back premierships in 1920 and 1921. Minogue then crossed to Hawthorn in 1926, and captained Hawthorn in the opening games of the season, after which he decided to retire because of injury. Minogue also was the only man to coach five League clubs: Richmond, Hawthorn, Carlton, St Kilda and Fitzroy. George Heinz captained Geelong for four games in 1910, but due to the outbreak of World War I and the anti-German feeling in the community, Heinz changed his name to Haines, and joined the army. He resumed his League career with Melbourne in 1919 and captained the club in 28 matches. Haines retired in 1925, but St Kilda coaxed him out of retirement two years later. He was appointed captain, but played only one game before hanging up the boots for good. And Len Thomas captained three clubs in three successive seasons, an unusual distinction. He led South Melbourne in twelve games in 1938; the next year he skippered Hawthorn 16 times, and the following season in 1940 he crossed to North Melbourne where he captained the side on six occasions.

• • •

They could be called Claytons captains, for five players have been appointed club captains for a season, but failed to play a game due to injury. They are: Bill Stuckey, Carlton, 1901; Brian Gleeson, St Kilda, 1957; Bob Skilton, South Melbourne, 1969; Neale Daniher, Essendon, 1982; and Michael Turner, Geelong, 1985.

• Quick Quiz •

1   Who captained Geelong in the 1963 Grand Final?

2   Which player captained Essendon in more than 200 matches?

3   Which League clubs were captained by Des Tuddenham?

4   Who was Brisbane's first captain?

5   Name the two men who have captained St Kilda in more than 100 matches.

6   Name the last League premiership captain who started the game on the bench.

7   Who captained Victoria against Western Australia in 1985 but was never captain of his club?

8   Who was the first captain of the West Coast Eagles?

9   Name the last captain to win the Brownlow medal.

10 Name North Melbourne's first premiership captain.

Answers

1   *Fred Wooller.*

2   *Dick Reynolds.*

3   *Collingwood and Essendon.*

4   *Mark Mickan.*

5   *Darrel Baldock and Danny Frawley.*

6   *Bruce Monteath (1980, Richmond).*

7   *Russell Greene (St Kilda and Hawthorn).*

8   *Ross Glendinning, 1987.*

9   *Barry Round (1981, South Melbourne).*

10   *Barry Davis, 1975.*

PLAYERS WHO HAVE CAPTAINED LEAGUE TEAMS IN 100 OR MORE MATCHES

Player	Career Span	Career Matches	Club	Matches as Captain
Reynolds, Dick	1938-50	320	Essendon	224
Whitten, Ted	1951-70	321	Footscray	212
Nicholls, John	1957-74	328	Carlton	187
Kernahan, Stephen	1986-94	199	Carlton	174
Bentley, Percy	1925-40	263	Richmond	168
Skilton, Bob	1956-68 1970-71	237	South Melbourne	165
Frawley, Danny	1984-94	226	St Kilda	163
Dyer, Jack	1931-49	312	Richmond	160
Murray, Kevin	1955-64 1967-74	333	Fitzroy	159
Coventry, Syd	1922-34	227	Collingwood	153
Arthur, Graham	1955-68	232	Hawthorn	153
Schimmelbusch, Wayne	1973-87	306	North Melbourne	150
Hickey, Reg	1926-40	245	Geelong	142
Tuddenham, Des	1962-71 1976-77	251	Collingwood	73
	1972-75		Essendon	69
Barassi, Ron	1953-64	254	Melbourne	92
	1965-69		Carlton	49
Tuck, Michael	1972-91	426	Hawthorn	139
Young, Henry	1897-1910	167	Geelong	137
Minogue, Dan	1911-16	180	Collingwood	41
	1920-25		Richmond	94
	1926		Hawthorn	1
Carroll, Dennis	1981-93	219	Sydney	131
Olliver, Arthur	1935-50	272	Footscray	127
Flower, Robert	1973-88	272	Melbourne	127
Daniher, Terry	1976-77	313	South Melbourne	
	1978-92		Essendon	127
Scott, Don	1967-81	302	Hawthorn	124
Shaw, Tony	1978-94	313	Collingwood	123
Hutchison, Bill	1942-57	290	Essendon	122
Roos, Paul	1982-94	269	Fitzroy	122
Clarke, Jack	1951-67	263	Essendon	121
Cubbins, Bill	1915 1919-26 1928-30	162	St Kilda	87
	1931-32		Footscray	32
	1934			
La Fontaine, Alan	1934-42 1945	171	Melbourne	119
Richardson, Wayne	1966-78	278	Collingwood	117
Matthews, Leigh	1969-85	332	Hawthorn	112
Davis, Barry	1961-72	289	Essendon	40
	1973-75		North Melbourne	71

PLAYERS WHO HAVE CAPTAINED LEAGUE TEAMS IN 100 OR MORE MATCHES (cont.)

Ruthven, Alan	1940-41 1943-54	222	Fitzroy	110
Nankervis, Ian	1967-83	325	Geelong	110
Kyne, Phonse	1934-44 1946-50	245	Collingwood	107
Clegg, Ron	1945-54 1956-60	231	South Melbourne	106
Baldock, Darrel	1962-68	119	St Kilda	104
Hughson, Fred	1938-47	164	Fitzroy	103
Rowe, Des	1946-57	176	Richmond	103
Matthews, Herbie	1932-45	191	South Melbourne	101
Foote, Les	1941-51 1954-55	165	North Melbourne St. Kilda	101
Williams, Mark	1981-86 1987-90	201	Collingwood Brisbane	100 12

The Tacticians

John Worrall has a lot to answer for. Worrall started the whole coaching merry-go-round when he became the game's first official coach in 1906. Worrall led Carlton to the flag that year, and created the position that is the most important in the game today. Despite the fact that coaching is not a long-term profession (although there have been a few exceptions), it's never short of applicants. The coach accepts his lot with his head always on the chopping block.

Coaches seem to age before their time, and if the hair doesn't fall out it turns grey! This must say something about the stress of the job. Even success doesn't guarantee job security, for on occasion premiership coaches have been sacked before the cup has had time to tarnish.

But after playing, coaching is the next best thing. It's in the blood of most players.

• • •

There have been only three cases where fathers and their sons have coached League teams. Charlie Pannam coached Richmond in 1912; his son Charlie jnr coached South Melbourne in 1923 through to 1928; and his younger son Alby also coached Richmond between 1953 and 1955. Bill Thomas coached South Melbourne in 1910 and 1911; his son, Len, guided Hawthorn in 1939, and in 1940 took over North Melbourne for the first twelve games of the season. Percy Rowe steered the ship at Fitzroy in 1935 and Carlton in 1937; his son Des coached Richmond in 54 matches in a three-year stint from 1953 to 1955.

• • •

It was a significant victory when St Kilda defeated Melbourne in Round 9, 1965 at the MCG by 61 points, for it was the first time Norm Smith as coach of the Demons had experienced a 10-goal defeat since taking over the reigns in 1952. It took 267 attempts for an opposing team to achieve that feat.

• • •

Charlie Clymo has a unique League coaching record. He guided Geelong to a premiership in his first year of coaching in 1931. Clymo then shocked the Cats by turning his back on League football and returning to country coaching the next year.

• • •

Glenn Hawker played under three different League coaches in three consecutive senior games. Hawker played for Essendon in the last home and away round under Kevin Sheedy in 1988. The following year, he crossed to Carlton and played the opening game of the season under Blues boss Robert Wall. Injury then interrupted his season, and by the time he made it back to the Seniors in Round 16, Alex Jesaulenko was coach of Carlton, replacing the sacked Walls.

• • •

Only three men have reached the top of the coaching tree in three major state competitions: Victoria, South Australia and Western Australia. They are Allan Killigrew who coached St Kilda, Norwood and Subiaco; Dennis Jones, who coached Melbourne, Central Districts, West Perth; and Graham Campbell who coached Fitzroy, Glenelg and West Perth.

• • •

Alan Joyce in his first year as coach of a League club led Hawthorn to the 1988 premiership. The following year Allan Jeans returned to coach the Hawks after recovering from illness, and guided the club to another flag. That was the first time a League club had won back-to-back flags under different coaches.

• • •

Alex Jesaulenko had three separate coaching stints. He coached Carlton between 1978 and 1979, then moved to St Kilda and led the Saints between 1980 and 1982, before coaching the Blues again in 1989 and 1990. Amazingly, each of 'Jezza's' coaching appointments was made after the season had started. In 1978, in Round 7, replacing Ian Stewart at Carlton; in 1980, in Round 3, replacing Mike Patterson at St Kilda; and in 1989, Round 11, replacing Robert Walls at Carlton.

• • •

There have been three incidents in League football of joint coaches being appointed. The first time was in 1917 when Herb Howson and Henry Elms coached South Melbourne. In 1939, Jack Baggott* resigned as coach at Essendon during the season, and Vic Reynolds and Harry Hunter were appointed off-field and on-field coaches for the remainder of the season. And in 1940, Len Thomas resigned as coach of North Melbourne due to military service after Round 12, and his replacements were Jim Adamson and Wally Carter.

*   *Jack Baggott passed away in June 1995, aged 88 years.*

• • •

When Ted 'E.J.' Whitten was appointed coach to replace the sacked Charlie Sutton at Footscray in July 1957, he became the youngest ever League coach. E.J. was just 14 days short of his 24th birthday when he fired up his charges for the first time. And at 27 years and 206 days, Allan Jeans is the youngest non-playing coach in League history. He first took control of St Kilda for the opening round of 1961, and in 1966 coached that club to its only premiership.

• • •

Don McKenzie holds a unique record in League football. McKenzie played with Footscray's Under-19s, Reserves and Seniors. He also coached the Bulldogs at all three levels.

• • •

Collingwood's Jock McHale easily holds the record as the oldest person to coach in a League game. McHale was 66 years 295 days old when he coached the Magpies for the last time. The occasion was the 1949 First Semi-final against Essendon at the MCG. Next in line is John Kennedy, who was 59 years 245 days old when he gave his last rev-up to his North Melbourne players against Sydney under lights at the MCG on 1 September 1989. And Allan Jeans was 58 years 342 days old when he guided Richmond to victory over Sydney at the SCG in the last home and away game of the 1992 season.

• • •

In the pressure cooker of a League game, the coach on occasion has to have a smile and crack the odd joke to keep himself sane, along with his fellow selectors. One such moment comes quickly to my mind, during the time I was coaching Richmond:

The Tigers were playing Geelong in 1990 down at Kardinia Park. Richmond hadn't won at Cat Land since Jack Dyer was a boy, and Geelong was the redhot favourite. The year before, Geelong lost the grand final by a kick, while the Tigers won the wooden spoon. The critics had the Cats as unbackable favourites, and on radio before the match, famous radio broadcaster Bill Jacobs gave co-commentator John 'Sam' Newman odds of a million to one on Richmond winning the game. Newman, very confidently, put a dollar on the Tigers. Before the game, I wrote on the blackboard each critic's tips for the match; some thirty-odd experts all picked Geelong by huge margins. I pointed out only Michael Roach had selected Richmond to win in the magazine *Inside Football*. 'But we must remember he played for the club,' I told the players, but then again I'm told he even tossed up whether to pick the Cats.

The coach's box in those days at Kardinia park put the coach right amongst the supporters — so close you could pat them on the head. Unfortunately, they could hear everything that was said, so every time I relayed a message to my runner, they would yell out the move in advance. Suffice to say, this drove me mad, and this went on all day. But on the other side of the coin, I could hear everything they said as well, and they criticised Geelong star Paul Couch all day for handballing and not kicking the ball. Couch had a crook ankle, and refused to kick the ball, forcing him to get caught on a number of occasions. This drove the Cats supporters crazy. With only a few minutes to go in the game, Richmond had caused a massive upset, and,with the siren about to go, the Tigers had no chance of losing the game. I picked up the phone and in my loudest voice said to my runner, 'For Christ's sake, would you go out and tell Paul Couch to kick the bloody ball; he's driving us all mad'. The Geelong contingency in front of the coach's box all turned around and said 'Y-e-e-s-s' and pumped their arms into the air. It was the only time I sent a message out to an opposing player.

• • •

Quarter-time during the 1980 Qualifying Final at Waverley produced an amazing scene. Carlton coach Peter 'Percy' Jones (who once ran for parliament under the slogan 'Point Percy to Parliament'!) and Richmond coach Tony Jewell were both fired up as they broke away from addressing their respective sides at the first break. This was because just before time-on in the first quarter the Blues' dynamic smallman Ken Sheldon, while impersonating Rudolph Nureyev by dancing around the Tiger's defence, was cleaned up by Tiger's backman Graeme Landy and was stretchered off the ground. An all-out mêlée started that boiled over to the break. As both coaches were leaving the arena, Jones ventured close to the Jewell camp and verbally clashed with Dr Rudy Webster, who was the Tigers' sports psychologist and who had previously been associated with Carlton. Jewell became agitated with Jones' comments and ran 15 metres, pushing Jones in the chest. A couple of wild punches from both coaches missed their mark and neither was in danger of being hurt. Officials from both clubs raced in and dragged them away. Both were talking to each other whilst being restrained, but through their walrussed moustaches neither could decipher what the other was saying. Richmond won the match and the coaches' brawl was declared a draw.

• • •

Tom Hafey and David Parkin are the only two men to have coached three different clubs into finals. Hafey achieved it with Richmond in 1967, '69, '71, '72, '73, '74 and '75, with Collingwood in 1977, '78, '79, '80 and '81, and with Sydney in 1986 and '87. Parkin achieved it with Hawthorn in 1977 and '78, Carlton in 1981, '82, '83, '84, '85, with Fitzroy in 1986, and again with Carlton in '93 and '94.

• • •

The Carlton coaching position could be described as a merry-go-round when one talks about Alex Jesaulenko and David Parkin. Jesaulenko coached Carlton in 1978 to the end of 1979 when he was replaced by Peter 'Percy' Jones. Parkin then replaced Jones and held the top job from 1981 through to 1985. Robert Walls then replaced Parkin and guided the Blues from 1986 to 1989, whereupon Walls was sacked mid-season and replaced by Jesaulenko who held the top job until the end of 1990. He was then dumped for Parkin, who has held the reigns since 1991.

• • •

It was a big game, Geelong versus Melbourne at the MCG, and Geelong coach Tommy Hafey put into place his meticulous plan to win the game. He assembled his players at Kardinia Park before heading to Melbourne as a unit. They counted the heads and one player was missing — star forward Gary Ablett.

So some phone calls were made and some extra time was given, but when the champ didn't show up Hafey set the team on the road. The coaches had organized a brunch for the players at the MCG in the rooms and at 11pm the players tucked into the food as Hafey outlined team strategies, moves as well as the strengths and weaknesses of the Melboune side. Behind the scenes, officials were worried about Ablett and continued to try to make contact with their champion. Hafey then introduced several motivational films to rev-up his players. Still the search went on for Gary Ablett. The players then stripped and went into their footy game routines, having rub-downs, while Hafey walked around talking to players about the roles they were going to play on an individual basis.

Being a man short, Hafey then dragged Damian Drum, who was playing in the Reserves, from the ground to replace Ablett in the starting line-up. Officials were concerned the great player may have had an accident and continued their search making phone calls and enquiries. Drum was told that after nearly playing a full game in the Reserves he would have to sit on the bench and then have a shower and freshen-up for another afternoon of action.

At 1.25pm as the players were going through their stretching exercises and ball-handling routines the door swung open. The great man walked in with his bag. Car trouble was the reason given for the very, very late arrival, only a half an hour before game time. Club officials madly wanted action and asked Hafey to leave Ablett out of the team for disciplinary reasons. They said that they could not contact him, there'd been no contact with them, and that the team has to be shown some strength.

Hafey replied 'What?! Leave Gary Ablett out of the team? You've gotta be joking! The man's a champion! His car's only broken down, that's all!'

The officials then said that at least he should be sat on the bench to show some resolve that a player just can't turn up late for a game.

Hafey again replied 'What? Sit Gary Ablett on the bench?! You've gotta be kidding! The man's a champion!'

The coach got his way. Ablett started on the half-forward flank and according to Hafey booted five goals in the first quarter, nine goals for the day and was unanimously best on the ground. So much for preparation!

• • •

It's not always easy to find a job for a player and most clubs always like to have players in work. Tom Hafey, who coached four clubs — Richmond, Collingwood, Geelong, and Sydney — was always a stickler that players need to have a job to complement their football career. To protect the innocent we won't give the name of the player or the club, but Tom Hafey approached a fanatical club supporter who had a very large landscaping business and enjoyed employing members of the club, and asked him to take on a player who was out of work. The duties at the landscaping job were simple ones such as doing some mowing, cleaning up around lawns, doing a bit of planting and just general maintenance in keeping certain properties under control and looking very nice. So a job was organized for 'the player' who had become disinterested in his previous job, that being the job of a storeman.

To Hafey's surprise, the fanatical supporter came to him after only a couple of weeks and nearly in tears announced he would have to sack the player for he was unable to carry out the simplest of duties and seemed disinterested. A meeting therefore was quickly arranged with the player, Hafey and the club officials to see what line of employment would satisfy him. The club explained how they wanted the player to have a job, and could he tell them exactly what he wanted and was looking for, for it was important that he be happy in his occupation so that he could play good football.

The player sat there in front of Hafey and the officials and said in the most serious and studious manner that after giving it a lot of thought there was one job that he'd always dreamed about and one job that he would love to do but had never ever been given the opportunity... The officials and Hafey urged him to give them some insight in what he wanted to be so they could go out and help him find this job of his choice. The player then finally said 'What I want to be is an astronaut.' As the jaws of the officials dropped, and they looked at one another in amazement, Hafey took control and said 'I don't know how many jobs there are for astronauts around this place. But I tell you what, I'll make some enquiries and I'll get back to you.'

• • •

When should a coach worry and when should he just relax?

Malcolm Blight in his days coaching Geelong had one such afternoon. The Cats were at home to Essendon,coached by the unpredictable Kevin Sheedy and Derek Kickett was in full flight. His brilliant display in the centre was causing Blight to lose more of his hair. Paul Couch, Garry Hocking and his brother Steven had all been given a crack at Kickett in the first half with no success. Kickett was simply unstoppable. With the game conceivably slipping away Blight and his co-selectors met at half-time and shuffled the team around in another effort to curb Kickett's exceptional display. He pointed out in his half-time address the changes and why they had to be made to stop the mercurial match winner.

Taking up his position in the coach's box after the main break Blight scanned the field for any Sheedy positional changes. He rubbed his eyes, blinked, took another look and then slumped back into his seat. There was Kickett playing in the back pocket!

• • •

It took father figure coach Tom Hafey more than five years to guide his team to victory over pupil coach Kevin Sheedy. The two were first opposed as coaches in Round 8, 1981, when Essendon defeated Collingwood at Waverley Park. Finally, in Round 11, 1986, Sydney, led by Hafey, defeated Sheedy's Bombers at Windy Hill by 20 points.

• Quick Quiz •

1   Who coached Collingwood to the 1958 premiership?

2   In which season did Ron Barassi first coach North Melbourne?

3   Name the two League playing coaches who officiated in 1981.

4   Which League clubs were coached by Bill Stephen?

5   Who was West Coast's first coach?

6   Who took over as coach of the Brisbane Bears after Peter Knights was sacked as coach?

7   Name the only Collingwood coach to lead the Magpies to a wooden spoon.

8   Who replaced Tom Hafey as coach of Collingwood.

9   In the last 50 years, who has coached senior League clubs but never played League football?

10   In 1991, Queensland defeated Victoria in interstate football at the 'Gabba. Name the coaches?

Answers

1   *Phonse Kyne*

2   *1973*

3   *Malcolm Blight (North Melbourne) and Alex Jesaulenko (St Kilda).*

4   *Fitzroy and Essendon.*

5   *Ron Alexander.*

6   *Paul Feltham.*

7   *Murray Weideman, 1976.*

8   *Mick Erwin, 1982.*

9   *Alan Miller (1967–68, South Melbourne), Col Kinnear (1989–91, Sydney), John Todd (1988–89, West Coast), Bob Hammond (1984, part of season, Sydney), John Cahill (1983–84, Collingwood), Hugh Thomas (1944–45, St Kilda).*

10   *Norm Dare (Queensland), Rod Austin (Victoria).*

COACHES OF PREMIERSHIP TEAMS AT TWO OR MORE CLUBS 1897-1994

Coach	Teams	Season
Jack Worrall	Carlton	1906-07-08
	Essendon	1911-12
'Checker' Hughes	Richmond	1932
	Melbourne	1939-40-41, 1948
Percy Bentley	Richmond	1934
	Carlton	1945, 1947
Ron Barassi	Carlton	1968, 1970
	North Melbourne	1975, 1977
David Parkin	Hawthorn	1978
	Carlton	1981-82
Allan Jeans	St Kilda	1966
	Hawthorn	1963, 1986, 1989

YOUNGEST COACHES

Coach	Club	Season	Age
Bentley, P.*	Richmond	1934	27 years, 304 days
Reynolds, D.**	Essendon	Round 9, 1939	23 years, 362 days
Reynolds, D.*	Essendon	1942	27 years, 91 days
Dyer, J.*	Richmond	1943	29 years, 314 days
Whitten, T.**	Footscray	Round 13, 1957	23 years, 351 days
Jeans, A.	St Kilda	Round 1, 1961	27 years, 206 days
Murray, K.**	Fitzroy	Round 1, 1963	24 years, 306 days
Gellie, G.	St Kilda	Round 19, 1984	29 years, 228 days.

* *Denotes Premiership Coaches*
** *Denotes Playing coaches*

BROTHERS WHO WERE LEAGUE COACHES

Coach	Team/s	Season
Norm Smith	Fitzroy	1949-51
	Melbourne	1952-67
	South Melbourne	1969-72
Len Smith	Fitzroy	1958-62
	Richmond	1964-65
Bob Rose	Collingwood	1964-71
		1985-86
	Footscray	1972-75
Kevin Rose	Fitzroy	1975-77

AFL COACHES WHO ACHIEVED A PREMIERSHIP IN THEIR FIRST SEASON

Coach	Team/s	Season
Charlie Ricketts	South Melbourne	1909
John Worrall	Essendon	1911
Percy Parratt	Fitzroy	1913
Henry Howson	South Melbourne	1918
Danny Minogue	Richmond	1920
Vic Belcher	Fitzroy	1922
Cliff Rankin	Geelong	1925
Charlie Clymo	Geelong	1931
Jack Bissett	South Melbourne	1933
Percy Bentley	Richmond	1934
Brighton Diggins	Carlton	1938
John Nicholls	Carlton	1972
David Parkin	Carlton	1981
Alan Joyce	Hawthorn	1988

COACHES TO EXPERIENCE THE HIGHS AND LOWS

The following men were in charge when their teams won Premierships and 'Wooden Spoons'.

Coach	Premierships	Wooden Spoons
Reg Hickey	Geelong 1937, 1951, 1952	Geelong 1957, 1958
Charlie Sutton	Footscray 1954	Footscray 1967
Norm Smith	Melbourne 1955-56-57, 1959-60, 1964	South Melbourne 1971
Ron Barassi	Carlton 1968, 1970	Melbourne 1981
	Nth Melbourne 1975, 1977	Sydney 1993-94
Tony Jewell	Richmond 1980	St Kilda 1983
		Richmond 1987
Dan Minogue	Richmond 1920-21	Hawthorn 1927
Robert Walls	Carlton 1987	Brisbane 1991

LEAGUE COACHES OF 200 MATCHES OR MORE

Coach	Team	Career Span	Seasons	Total Matches	Wins	Losses	Ties	P/ships
Jock McHale	Collingwood	1912-49	38	714	467	237	10	8
Allan Jeans	St Kilda	1961-76	16	332	193	138	1	1
	Hawthorn	1981-87 1989-90	9	221	159	61	1	3
	Richmond	1992	1	22	5	17	0	0
	Total:		**26**	**575**	**357**	**216**	**2**	**4**
Tom Hafey	Richmond	1966-76	11	248	173	73	2	4
	Collingwood	1977-82	6	138	89	47	2	0
	Geelong	1983-85	3	66	31	35	0	0
	Sydney	1986-88	3	70	43	27	0	0
	Total:		**23**	**522**	**336**	**182**	**4**	**4**
Ron Barassi	Carlton	1965-71	7	147	99	47	1	2
	Nth Melbourne	1973-80	8	198	129	66	3	2
	Melbourne	1981-85	5	110	33	77	0	0
	Sydney	1993-94	2	37	5	32	0	0
	Total:		**22**	**492**	**266**	**222**	**4**	**4**
Norm Smith	Fitzroy	1949-51	3	55	30	23	2	0
	Melbourne	1952-67	16	310	198	107	5	6
	Sth Melbourne	1969-72	4	87	26	61	0	0
	Total:		**23**	**452**	**254**	**191**	**7**	**6**

LEAGUE COACHES OF 200 MATCHES OR MORE (cont.)

Dick Reynolds	Essendon	1939-60	22	420	277	137	6	0
Percy Bentley	Richmond	1934-40	7	133	86	46	1	1
	Carlton	1941-55	15	281	167	110	4	2
	Total:		**22**	**414**	**253**	**156**	**5**	**3**
John Kennedy	Hawthorn	1960-63 1967-76	14	296	181	113	2	3
	Nth Melbourne	1985-89	5	113	55	55	3	0
	Total:		**19**	**409**	**238**	**168**	**5**	**3**
'Checker' Hughes	Richmond	1927-32	6	120	87	31	2	1
	Melbourne	1933-41 1945-48 1965	14	254	157	95	2	4
	Total:		**20**	**374**	**244**	**126**	**4**	**5**
Dan Minogue	Richmond	1920-25	6	105	59	45	1	2
	Hawthorn	1926-27	2	36	4	31	1	0
	Carlton	1929-34	6	117	85	32	0	0
	St Kilda	1935-37	3	54	30	24	0	0
	Fitzroy	1940-42	3	51	25	26	0	0
	Total:		**20**	**363**	**203**	**158**	**2**	**2**
David Parkin	Hawthorn	1977-80	4	94	57	37	0	1
	Carlton	1981-85 1991-94	9	211	131	78	2	2
	Fitzroy	1986-88	3	69	30	39	0	0
	Total:		**16**	**374**	**218**	**154**	**2**	**3**
Reg Hickey	Geelong	1932 1936-40 1949-59	18	304	184	117	3	3
Kevin Sheedy	Essendon	1981-94	14	329	212	115	2	3
Robert Walls	Fitzroy	1981-85	5	115	60	54	1	0
	Carlton	1986-89	4	84	56	28	0	1
	Brisbane	1991-94	4	86	20	65	1	0
	Total:		**13**	**285**	**136**	**147**	**2**	**1**
Bob Rose	Collingwood	1964-71 1985-86	10	192	121	69	2	0
	Footscray	1972-75	4	89	42	45	2	0
	Total:		**14**	**281**	**163**	**114**	**4**	**0**
'Phonse' Kyne	Collingwood	1950-63	14	271	161	108	2	2

LEAGUE COACHES OF 200 MATCHES OR MORE (cont.)

Jack Worrall	Carlton	1902-09	8	144	100	43	1	3
	Essendon	1911-15 1918-19	7	123	60	3	0	
	Total:		**11**	**259**	**155**	**100**	**4**	**3**
Michael Malthouse	Footscray	1984-89	6	135	67	66	2	0
	West Coast	1990-94	5	124	88	34	2	2
	Total:		**11**	**258**	**155**	**100**	**4**	**2**
Bill Stephen	Fitzroy	1955-57 1965-70 1979-80	11	214	67	146	1	0
	Essendon	1976-77	2	44	16	27	1	0
	Total:		**13**	**259**	**83**	**173**	**2**	**0**
John Northey	Sydney	1985	1	22	6	16	0	0
	Melbourne	1986-92	7	167	90	76	1	0
	Richmond	1993-94	2	42	16	26	0	0
	Total:		**10**	**231**	**112**	**118**	**1**	**0**
Ted Whitten	Footscray	1957-66 1969-71	13	228	91	137	0	0
Jack Dyer	Richmond	1941-52	12	225	134	89	2	1
Norman Clark	Carlton	1912 1914-18 1920-22	9	150	102	42	6	2
	Richmond	1919	1	19	12	7	0	0
	St Kilda	1925-26	2	35	14	21	0	0
	Nth Melbourne	1931	1	10	0	10	0	0
	Total:		**13**	**214**	**128**	**80**	**6**	**2**
Wally Carter	Nth Melbourne	1948-53 1958-62	11	208	96	111	1	0
Leigh Matthews	Collingwood	1986-94	9	202	117	82	3	1

COACHES OF THREE OR MORE CLUBS

Coach	Team	Season
Dan Minogue	Richmond	1920-25 (Premiers 1920-21)
	Hawthorn	1926-27
	Carlton	1929-34
	St Kilda	1935-37
	Fitzroy	1940-42
Alex Hall	St Kilda	1906
	Melbourne	1907-09, 1912-14
	Richmond	1910
	Hawthorn	1925

COACHES OF THREE OR MORE CLUBS (cont.)

Norman Clark	Carlton	1912, 1914-18, 1920-22 (Premiers 1914-15)
	Richmond	1919
	St Kilda	1925-26
	Nth Melbourne	1931
Ron Barassi	Carlton	1965-71 (Premiers 1968, 1970)
	Nth Melbourne	1973-80 (Premiers 1975, 1977)
	Melbourne	1981-85
	Sydney	1993-94
Charlie Ricketts	Sth Melbourne	1909, 1912 (Premiers 1909)
	Richmond	1914-16
	St Kilda	1921
Frank Maher	Essendon	1925-27
	Fitzroy	1932
	Carlton	1935-36
Percy Parratt	Fitzroy	1913-16, 1920-21 (Premiers 1913, 1916)
	Carlton	1924
	Geelong	1935
Paddy Scanlan	Footscray	1927-28
	Sth Melbourne	1930-31
	Nth Melbourne	1935-37
Norm Smith	Fitzroy	1949-51
	Melbourne	1952-67 (Premiers 1955-56-57, 1959-60, 1964)
	Sth Melbourne	1969-72
Tom Hafey	Richmond	1966-76 (Premiers 1967, 1969, 1973-74)
	Collingwood	1977-82
	Geelong	1983-85
	Sydney	1986-88
David Parkin	Hawthorn	1977-80 (Premiers 1978)
	Carlton	1981-85, 1991-94 (Premiers 1981-82)
	Fitzroy	1986-88
Robert Walls	Fitzroy	1981-85
	Carlton	1986-89 (Premiers 1987)
	Brisbane	1991-94
Allan Jeans	St Kilda	1961-76 (Premiers 1966)
	Hawthorn	1981-87, 1989-90 (Premiers 1983, 1986, 1989)
	Richmond	1992
John Northey	Sydney	1985
	Melbourne	1986-92
	Richmond	1993-94

LEAGUE PLAYERS WHOSE CAREERS WERE GUIDED BY THE MOST COACHES

Player	Coaches	Year
Bill Picken	Neil Mann	1974
	Ron Richards	1974
	Murray Weideman	1975-76
	Tom Hafey	1977-82
	Mick Erwin	1982
	John Cahill	1983
	Ricky Quade	1984
	Tony Franklin	1984
	Bob Hammond	1984
	John Northey	1985
	Bob Rose	1986
	Leigh Matthews	1986
Rod Carter	Graham Donaldson	1974
	Graham Campbell	1974, 1978
	Kevin Rose	1975-77
	Bill Stephen	1979
	Ian Stewart	1980-81
	Ricky Quade	1982-84
	Tony Franklin	1984
	Bob Hammond	1984
	John Northey	1985
	Tom Hafey	1986-88
	Col Kinnear	1989-90
Bruce Doull	Ron Barassi	1969-71
	John Nicholls	1972-75
	Keith McKenzie	1972, 1975
	Ian Thorogood	1976-77
	Ian Stewart	1978
	Sergio Silvagni	1978
	Alex Jesaulenko	1978-79
	Peter Jones	1980
	David Parkin	1981-85
	Robert Walls	1986
Geoff Raines	Tom Hafey	1976
	Barry Richardson	1976-78
	Tony Jewell	1979-81
	Francis Bourke	1982
	John Cahill	1983-84
	Bob Rose	1985-86
	Kevin Sheedy	1986
	Peter Knights	1987-89
	Paul Feltham	1989

LEAGUE PLAYERS WHOSE CAREERS WERE GUIDED BY THE MOST COACHES (cont.)

John Annear	Tom Hafey	1981-82
	Mick Erwin	1982
	John Cahill	1983
	Mike Patterson	1984
	Paul Sproule	1985
	Tony Jewell	1986
	Ron Alexander	1987
	John Todd	1988-89
	Mick Malthouse	1990
Warwick Capper	Ricky Quade	1983-84
	Tony Franklin	1984
	Bob Hammond	1984
	John Northey	1985
	Tom Hafey	1986-87
	Peter Knights	1988-89
	Paul Feltham	1989
	Norm Dare	1990
	Col Kinnear	1991
David Cloke	Tom Hafey	1974-76
	Barry Richardson	1976-78
	Tony Jewell	1979-81
	Francis Bourke	1982
	John Cahill	1983-84
	Bob Rose	1985-86
	Leigh Matthews	1986-89
	Kevin Bartlett	1990-91
Peter Francis	Alex Jesaulenko	1979
	Peter Jones	1980
	David Parkin	1981
	Robert Walls	1981-83
	Michael Patterson	1984
	Paul Sproule	1985
	Tony Jewell	1986
	Kevin Sheedy	1987-88
David Murphy	Tony Franklin	1984
	Bob Hammond	1984
	John Northey	1985
	Tom Hafey	1986-88
	Col Kinnear	1989-91
	Gary Buckenara	1992-93
	Brett Scott	1993
	Ron Barassi	1993-94

PLAYERS WITH THE MOST MATCHES UNDER ONE COACH ONLY

Player	Team	Seasons	Coach	Matches
Gordon Coventry	Collingwood	1920-37	Jock McHale	306
Bill Hutchison	Essendon	1942-57	Dick Reynolds	290
Harry Collier	Collingwood	1926-40	Jock McHale	253
Phonse Kyne	Collingwood	1934-44 1946-49 1950	Jock McHale	238
Ross Smith	St Kilda	1961-72 1975	Allan Jeans	234
Syd Coventry	Collingwood	1922-34	Jock McHale	227
Kevin Bartlett	Richmond	1966-76	Tom Hafey	231
Charlie Dibbs	Collingwood	1924-35	Jock McHale	216
Dick Clay	Richmond	1966-76	Tom Hafey	213
Brian Mynott	St Kilda	1964-75	Allan Jeans	209
Ron Barassi	Melbourne	1953-64	Norm Smith	204

AFL COACHES COACHED BY TOM HAFEY 1976-94

Coach	Seasons as coach		Coaching matches	Matches pl. under Hafey
Ian Stewart	Sth Melbourne	1976-77 1979-81	111	77
	Carlton	1978	3	
Barry Richardson	Richmond	1976 1977-78	46	124
Mike Patterson	St Kilda	1978-80	46	58
	Richmond	1984	22	
Des Tuddenham	Sth Melbourne	1978	22	2

AFL COACHES COACHED BY TOM HAFEY 1976-94 (cont.)

Tony Jewell	Richmond	1979-81 1986-87	113	61
	St Kilda	1983-84	40	
Royce Hart	Footscray	1980-82	53	175
Kevin Sheedy	Essendon	1981-94	329	204
Francis Bourke	Richmond	1982-83	46	202
Mick Erwin	Collingwood	1982	12	21
Mick Malthouse	Footscray West Coast	1984-89 1990-94	135 124	9
John Northey	Sydney Melbourne Richmond	1985 1986-92 1993-94	22 167 42	85
Paul Sproule	Richmond	1985	22	86
Allan Davis	St Kilda	1987	4	3
Kevin Bartlett	Richmond	1988-91	88	231
Neil Balme	Melbourne	1993-94	45	115
Brett Scott	Sydney	1993	2	9
TOTALS			1,494	1,462

Thrillers and Thrashings

For a player, there is nothing worse than trudging off the ground after being thrashed. A no-contest game leaves a sick feeling in the stomach of all club personnel. It's hard to rationalize why a club on a particular day becomes non-competitive, and the criticism and jibes from supporters and the media only magnify the embarrassment. On these days, no amount of positional changes or oratory skills offered by the coach will have any effect on the game. And the opposition always seems to have too many players on the ground for it to be a fair contest.

But then there are the thrillers. To win a thriller, particularly when you have come from the unwinnable position, is a victory to savour. Again, it can be hard to explain how a side can play so badly for most of a game, and then produce a champion effort to win the game. All we can say most of the time is 'That's football!'

The two most famous draws in League football are the 1948 and 1977 drawn grand finals. In1948, woeful kicking by Essendon allowed Melbourne to snatch a draw. The Bombers took until halfway into the second term before scoring their first goal. At half-time, Essendon had 2 goals 15 on the board to Melbourne's 4 goals 5. The Bombers kicked straighter in the third term, placing 4 goals 5, and led by 12 points at the last break. But the inaccuracy continued, and Melbourne nearly grabbed victory with two late goals from Jack Mueller and Adrian 'Spud' Dullard later in the game, to make the scores level. With only seconds to go, Norm Smith of Melbourne played on from 40 metres out, but his kick went across the face of the goals and out of bounds. From the boundary throw-in, Smith again grabbed the ball, but his own teammate Don Cordner knocked the ball from his grasp. Smith was only a couple of metres out from goal, and in attempting to pick up the ball, slipped over and the ball was cleared by Essendon's Cecil 'Cec' Ruddell. The siren sounded with the game a draw, the first ever drawn grand final. The final score: Essendon 7 goals 27 (69) points; Melbourne 10 goals 9 (69) points. Melbourne easily won the replay, 13 goals 11 (89) to Essendon's 7 goals 8 (50).

• • •

It looked like Collingwood's flag in 1977 when the 'Pies led North Melbourne at three-quarter time by 27 points. Schimmelbusch of North Melbourne kicked a point early in the final term, then Daryl Sutton and Phil Baker brought the Kangaroos within 14 points after kicking truly. David Dench, who had been moved from full-back to centre half-forward for North, intercepted a Phil Manassa handball to kick North's third goal in seven minutes. Arnold Briedis then Dench kicked behinds to get North within 7 points. Dench was off-target for a behind, then Baker goaled and the scores were level. Both clubs then swapped behinds with minus scores to Ross 'Twiggy' Dunne of Collingwood and Xavier Tanner of North Melbourne. Then it was North's turn to look winners when John Byrne kicked a point and Baker from a great mark goaled to propel North Melbourne to a seven-point lead. Collingwood's Peter Moore missed an easy shot, and so there was only a kick in it. With less than 60 seconds to go, Bill Picken, down from the Magpies' defence, kicked a high ball to the front of the goal square, where Dunne took a great mark in a big pack of players. From 15 metres out, Dunne goaled and the scores were level. Collingwood attacked from the bounce, and the ball was on their half-forward line when the siren sounded for only the second-ever grand final draw. In the replay, North were comfortable winners by 27 points, the same score Collingwood led North Melbourne by at three-quarter time in the first grand final. North Melbourne, 21 goals 25 (151) points defeated Collingwood 19 goals 10 (124).

• • •

On Sunday, 9 June 1991, Adelaide met Fitzroy for the first time in a League match. The match took place under lights at Football Park. For most of the match the Lions were in control, being ahead on the scoreboard at each break. With seconds to play in the last quarter, the Crows had the ball on their half-forward line, trailing by three points. Incredibly, two highly doubtful free kicks were paid in quick succession to the home team, resulting in a goal to Rod Jameson and victory for the Crows.

• • •

Carlton hosted North Melbourne at Princes Park on Saturday, 5 June 1976. The home team led quite convincingly for most of the match. With only time on to play in the last quarter the Blues held a 13 point advantage. The last five minutes belonged to one man — brilliant North Melbourne forward, Malcolm Blight. Firstly, he booted a difficult goal from a 45-degree angle. Seconds later he marked on the boundary in the right-hand forward pocket and calmly brought up both flags with an excellent 'banana' kick. In a final act he marked midway between the left-hand half-forward flank and wing. As he went back for his kick the siren sounded, with his team still five points down. He released a booming 70-metre torpedo punt which was on target. The ball sailed through the middle post high, to give the Kangaroos an amazing victory by one point.

• • •

One of the greatest ever exhibitions of Australian football took place at Princes Park on Saturday 7 May 1989, when Hawthorn met Geelong. Every skill in the book was displayed in the first half by Geelong, when it established a lead in excess of 50 points at one stage. With strategic positional moves by Hawk coach, Allan Jeans, including the placement of regular back-pocket, Gary Ayres in the centre, the Brown and Golds perished and eventually out-played their opponents to nose ahead late in the last quarter. Neither team deserved to lose — in fact Geelong's score of 25 goals 13 (163) remains the highest losing total in League history. Hawthorn was victorious by eight points.

Opposite page: Collingwood has been involved in two drawn matches in the 1995 season to date, including this thrilling match in Round 12 against Footscray.

• • •

Geelong has been a high-scoring unit in recent seasons. No better example of its explosive forward action has been demonstrated than its match against Brisbane at Carrara on Sunday, 3 May 1992. The small crowd of 7645 was amazed as the Cats launched attack after attack, scoring seven, nine, and seven goals respectively in the first three quarters. At three-quarter time they accepted the challenge of establishing a new League record high score. By late in the last quarter they had equalled Fitzroy's 13-year-old record of 238 points. As the siren was about to sound Billy Brownless took one last set shot which resulted in a behind to give his team the record.

• • •

Western Oval is rarely a happy hunting ground for visiting teams, particularly on cold, windy, wet days. Carlton was certainly unhappy on Saturday, 2 June 1991, when late in the final quarter Footscray held a seven goal lead. Re-markably, the Blues had not managed a single goal to that stage. To the relief of all Carlton supporters, Mark Arceri broke the drought with a major with a little time left. Footscray 8 goals 9 (57) defeated Carlton 1 goal 10 (16).

• Quick Quiz •

1   Which team was defeated by 190 points in a match during the 1979 VFL season?

2   Name the two League seasons which have produced tied grand finals?

3   Who scored the winning behind for St Kilda in the dying moments of the 1966 Grand Final?

4   At which venue was the only tied match of 1994 played?

5   Which team won three consecutive matches by 100 points or more in 1989?

6   Carlton staged a great comeback to defeat Collingwood in the 1970 Grand Final by 10 points after being 44 points down at half-time. Ted Hopkins came on at half-time to kick four goals for the Blues. Who did he replace?

7   Name the club that was 94 points down against Fitzroy at three-quarter time in 1992, but still managed to kick 11 goals and 1 behind in the last quarter.

8   St Kilda came back from a final quarter deficit of 48 points to defeat Sydney in 1994 at the SCG. What did St Kilda win by and how many goals did Tony Lockett kick?

9   Collingwood and West Coast played a draw during the 1990 finals series at Waverley. Who was the West Coast player who kicked the point to draw the game?

10 Essendon in 1985 recorded the highest score kicked in the final quarter of a grand final. What was it?

Answers

1   *Melbourne.*

2   *1948 (Essendon and Melbourne) and 1977 (Collingwood and North Melbourne)*

3   *Barry Breen.*

4   *Waverley (St Kilda v Adelaide).*

5   *Geelong.*

6   *Bert Thornley.*

7   *Essendon.*

8   *1 point, Lockett kicked 11 goals.*

9   *Peter Sumich.*

10 *11 goals 3 behinds (69 points against Hawthorn).*

100-POINT MARGINS BETWEEN SAME TEAMS THREE TIMES IN SUCCESSION 1897-1994

Year	Match	Round	Winning Margin
1982	**Essendon** v Footscray	1	109
		22	146
1983	**Essendon** v Footscray	6	132
1991	**Geelong** v Brisbane	4	102
		22	146
1992	**Geelong** v Brisbane	7	164

Round 20 in 1992 produced three 100-point wins — the most in one round in AFL history. Total number of 100-point wins 1897–1994 — 178.

ONE-POINT WINS IN FINALS MATCHES

Elimination final, 1986 — **Fitzroy** 8.10 (58) v Essendon 8.9 (57)
First semi-final, 1981 — **Collingwood** 19.19 (133) v Fitzroy 19.18 (132)
Second semi-final, 1965 — **St Kilda** 13.24 (102) v Collingwood 14.17 (101)
Preliminary final — **North Melbourne** 10.7 (67) v Carlton 9.12 (66)
Grand Final, 1947 — **Carlton** 13.8 (86) v Essendon 11.19 (85);
1966, **St Kilda** 10.14 (74) v Collingwood 10.13 (73)

Round 13 in 1938 produced four one-point wins — the most in one round in AFL history. Total number of one-point wins 1897–1994 — 242.

MATCH-WINNING GOALS KICKED AFTER FINAL SIREN

Year	Match	Player
1967	**Geelong** v Collingwood	Bill Ryan
1973	**North Melbourne** v Collingwood	Doug Wade
1976	**North Melbourne** v Carlton	Alan Stoneham
1987	**North Melbourne** v Melbourne	Alastair Clarkson
	Carlton v North Melbourne	Stephen Kernahan
	Hawthorn v Melbourne	Gary Buckenara
1991	**Adelaide** v Fitzroy	Rod Jameson

CLUBS IN TWO TIED MATCHES IN ONE SEASON 1897-1994

1909	Collingwood		Fitzroy	1952	Carlton
1911	Carlton	1935	Footscray	1960	Richmond
1914	Carlton		Collingwood	1972	Carlton
1921	Melbourne	1944	Essendon	1977	St Kilda
	Carlton		St Kilda	1980	St Kilda
	Essendon	1951	Fitzroy		

Total number of tied matches 1897–1994 — 117.

100-POINT WINS BY A CLUB IN CONSECUTIVE ROUNDS 1897-1994

Year	Round	Winning Margin	Match
1981	12	100	**Geelong** v St Kilda
	13	114	**Geelong** v North Melbourne
1987	16	130	**Sydney** v West Coast
	17	163	**Sydney** v Essendon
1989	7	119	**Geelong** v St Kilda
	8	129	**Geelong** v Brisbane
	9	134	**Geelong** v Richmond
1992	7	164	**Geelong** v Brisbane
	8	123	**Geelong** v Adelaide

100-POINT WINS IN FINALS MATCHES

First semi-final, 1969 — **Richmond** 25.17 (167) v Geelong 7.7 (49)
Preliminary final, 1984 — **Essendon** 28.6 (174) v Collingwood 5.11 (41)
Elimination final, 1987 — **Melbourne** 22.26 (158) v North Melbourne 5.10 (40)

100-POINT MARGINS BETWEEN SAME TEAMS TWICE IN ONE SEASON 1897–1994

Year	Match	Round	Winning Margin
1899	**Geelong** v St. Kilda	14	117
		17	161
1980	**Richmond** v Footscray	5	118
		18	115
1982	**Essendon** v Footscray	1	109
		22	146
1991	**Hawthorn** v Fitzroy	6	157
		17	126
	Geelong v Brisbane	4	102
		19	101

TIED MATCHES IN CONSECUTIVE WEEKS

1911	Carlton v Essendon
	Carlton v South Melbourne
1921	Carlton v Fitzroy
	Carlton v South Melbourne
1956	Carlton v St Kilda
	Hawthorn v South Melbourne

TIED MATCHES ON THE SAME DAY

1911	Carlton v South Melbourne
	Geelong v Melbourne
1914	Collingwood v Carlton
	Geelong v Essendon
1921	St Kilda v Melbourne
	South Melbourne v Carlton
1944	St Kilda v Essendon
	Richmond v Footscray
1977	Essendon v Richmond
	St Kilda v South Melbourne

* On 26 May 1973, both the Reserves and Seniors matches between North Melbourne and Footscray resulted in a tie — the only such case in AFL history.

CLUB IN MOST TIED MATCHES – CONSECUTIVE SEASONS

Geelong v Richmond, 1960
      v North Melbourne, 1961
      v Carlton, 1962
      v Hawthorn, 1963
      v Essendon, 1964

CLUB IN LEAST TIED MATCHES – CONSECUTIVE SEASONS

Geelong v Essendon, 1969
      v Essendon, 1987

Badges of Honour

The Brownlow medal was first awarded in 1924. It carries the name of former Geelong football club administrator Charles Brownlow and has always been decided on by the votes of the umpire. In the early days the winner was notified by the League without fanfare, and it didn't carry the prestige that the medal does today. The League later allowed the medal count to be broadcast on radio and then turned it into a gala TV occasion with invited players in attendance. On a number of occasions the Brownlow winner has not won his club's best and fairest award in the same year, but despite controversy and criticism the medal remains the highest individual award in the game.

On 29 October 1980, the AFL board of directors decided that players finishing with equal votes would each receive a Brownlow medal and would not be subjected to a countback. In 1981, Fitzroy's Bernie Quinlan and South Melbourne's Barry Round created history when they each received a medal. But it wasn't until 1989 that the League decided to recognize those players previously on a countback, so at a presentation at the Southern Cross on 8 August, more medals were presented. The recipients were Harry Collier, Collingwood; Allan Hopkins, Footscray; Des Fothergill, Collingwood; Col Austen, Hawthorn; Verdun Howell, St Kilda; Herbie Matthews, South Melbourne; Noel Teasdale, North Melbourne; and Bill Hutchison, Essendon — all worthy winners of the Brownlow medal.

• • •

Harry Collier was awarded the 1930 Brownlow medal retrospectively, but in 1938 he received the biggest suspension handed out to a Brownlow medallist. Collier was reported for striking Carlton wingman Jack Carney. Collier had an unblemished record over his 13-year career, and expected a sentence of one or two games after pleading guilty to the charge. But the Tribunal shocked the football world and stunned Collier by rubbing him out for 14 matches. The VFL was swamped by protests, and a petition with 2500 names calling for a rehearing was presented to the League. But Collier's sentence stood, and he missed the grand final that saw his beloved Magpies go down to Carlton, by 15 points.

• • •

Since the inception of the Brownlow medal in 1924, only six winners have never played in a finals series. The champion players who have never had the thrill and the honour of running out in a finals game are triple Brownlow medallist, Fitzroy's Haydn Bunton, who won the medal in 1931, '32, and '35; teammate Wilfred 'Chicken' Smallhorn, the 1933 winner, and fellow Fitzroy star Dinny Ryan who won in 1936. The other three players to make up the unique group are St Kilda's Colin Watson, 1924; South Melbourne's Fred Goldsmith, 1955, and St Kilda's Brian Gleeson, the winner in 1957.

• • •

In 1933, Fitzroy champion Wilfred 'Chicken' Smallhorn became the first winner of the Brownlow medal to have the time-honoured award presented to him in public. The ceremony was performed at the MCG on the first semi-final day, when Geelong beat Carlton. Thirty-seven years later, the VFL decided to conduct a Brownlow medal count at a public function at the Dallas Brooks Hall in Melbourne. Previously the count had taken place at Harrison

House, the League headquarters at the time, and was not open to the public or players. Channel 7 for the first time also had a direct telecast of the event, and with all fancied players invited, it also meant the media for the first time had direct access to the winner. South Melbourne champion Peter Bedford won the first televised medal, polling 25 votes, beating Footscray star Gary Dempsey and Carlton champion Alex Jesaulenko.

• • •

The 1987 Brownlow count was held at the Hyatt on Collins, and the two favourites on the big night were Saint's star Tony Lockett and Hawthorn's dynamo John Platten. But after only eight rounds had been counted, Carlton's Paul Meldrum had bolted, and was a run-away leader polling five best on ground performances, and with 15 votes said 'catch me if you can'. Unfortunately for Meldrum, he failed to register another vote, finishing equal second behind Lockett and Platten who tied with 20 votes. Under the old countback system, Lockett would have won the medal, polling four best on ground to Platten's three.

• • •

From the day he made his debut in 1963 with St Kilda, Ian Harlow Stewart was a champion. Combining with fellow Taswegian Darrel Baldock, Stewart spearheaded St Kilda to their first and only premiership in 1966. The year before he had won his first Brownlow medal and he made it a premiership Brownlow double when he took the medal for a second time in 1966. After a falling out with the Saints, Stewart moved to Richmond, where he again won the Brownlow, joining Haydn Bunton, Dick Reynolds and Bob Skilton as the only triple medal winners in League history. By playing in the Tiger's 1973 premiership side, he achieved a unique double: a Brownlow medal and a premiership at different clubs.

• • •

At the 1986 Brownlow medal dinner, Hawthorn's flamboyant wingman Robert DiPierdomenico claimed he only went along to the Southern Cross for a free feed. But by the end of the night the 'Big Dipper' had created history by becoming Hawthorn's first ever Brownlow medallist, when he tied for the covetted award with Sydney's Greg Williams. Both players polled 17 votes, the lowest tally to win the medal since the award was decided on a 3-2-1 count. Had the medal been decided on the old countback system, DiPierdomenico would have won, for he polled four best on ground performances, while Williams polled three. Later, retrospective Brownlows were awarded, and Col Austen became Hawthorn's first ever winner in 1949.

• • •

In the history of the Brownlow medal since the 3-2-1 system of voting to decide the winner was introduced in 1931, only on seven occasions has the winner polled less than 20 votes. Fitzroy's Wilfred 'Chicken' Smallhorn was the first in 1933 when he scored eighteen; Essendon's triple Brownlow winner, Dick Reynolds, twice won the award polling eighteen and nineteen votes in 1934 and 1938. Another Lion great, Kevin Murray, with 19, took the medal in 1969. Dual winners, Robert DiPierdomenico and Sydney's Greg Williams received 17 votes in 1986, and in 1990 Footscray's Tony Liberatore won the covetted award with 18 votes.

• • •

In October of 1980, when the VFL directors decided the countback system of splitting tied votes for the Brownlow was unfair and decided to award joint medals, the timing was perfect for former Footscray players, Bernie Quinlan and Barry Round. They each polled 22 votes to share the award. Quinlan of course was now a champion goalkicker for Fitzroy, and Round South Melbourne's top ruckman. Both were great mates, having started their careers together in the Latrobe Valley before joining Footscray.

• • •

Richmond's Geoff Raines was the big tip on the eve of the 1980 Brownlow medal count. The champion Tiger centreman had had a magnificent season, one that saw him win the Tiger's best and fairest award, the Jack Dyer medal, for the second time. But on Brownlow night he failed to win one Brownlow vote for the year. Unperturbed, Raines came out in the grand final a few days later against Collingwood and played another outstanding game, picking up 36 possessions. Raines later played for Collingwood and Essendon before finishing his career with the Brisbane Bears.

• • •

After Round 12 of the 1989 season, AFL investigation officer, Max Croxford, was called in to probe an incident involving Geelong champion and Brownlow medal favourite Gary Ablett. It was decided Ablett had a charge to answer for striking Melbourne player Gary Lyon. At the Tribunal hearing, Ablett said his faith in God had forced him to tell the truth, and he pleaded guilty to the charge. He told the Tribunal he had for the past years given his life to Jesus Christ, and deeply regretted what he did to Lyon. The Tribunal suspended Ablett for three matches, making him ineligible to win the Brownlow medal.

• • •

In 1976, Essendon ruckman Graham Moss won the Brownlow medal, polling 16 votes more than any previous winner. It was a unique year in Brownlow medal history, one with a twist, because for the first time each field umpire voted three, two and one — a combined twelve votes per game. Moss recorded 48 votes to become the first West Australian to win the covetted award. His record was shortlived, for the following year South Melbourne's Graham Teasdale polled 59 votes to win the medal. In 1978, the League reverted back to just 6 votes per game, as it is today.

• • •

Fitzroy coach Bernie Quinlan is one of the game's most decorated players. Quinlan played 366 matches, kicking 815 goals, for Footscray and Fitzroy, winning the Brownlow medal in 1981 and the John Coleman medal in 1983 and '84. But surprisingly, Quinlan never won a club best and fairest award. Another great player, Michael Tuck (the game's record-holder with 426 games and 320 goals) also never won a best and fairest at Hawthorn. It must be said, though, that he was runner-up on eight occasions. And Wayne Schimmelbusch, regarded as one of North Melbourne's greatest ever players and club games record-holder (306 games and 354 goals), also missed out on his club's highest honour.

• • •

Mention the name Alistair Lord, and one of the most unusual Tribunal hearings springs to mind. In 1962, Lord was starring for Geelong in the centre, and was a hot pick for the Brownlow medal. Then the unthinkable happened: The ball-playing Alistair was reported for striking Richmond utility Basil Moloney. Playing in the same match on the same side was Alistair's twin brother Stewart, who came forward as the culprit who had struck Moloney and not his brother. The claim was the umpire had got the twins mixed up. Alistair was exonerated, and went on to win the medal easily, polling 28 votes. But today, the issue is still a contentious one among football fans: Was it Alistair, or was it Stewart, who really struck Basil Moloney?

• • •

Position maketh the man: In the early '70s, Graham Teasdale was a star young forward with Richmond Under-19s and Reserves, but struggled to break into the senior team and hold a permanent spot due to the likes of Royce Hart and Neil Balme. In all, he played six games and booted 14 goals. The Tigers, in a sensational recruiting coup in 1975, grabbed South Melbourne star John Pitura in exchange for Brian Roberts, Francis Jackson, and the young Teasdale. Teasdale had early success with South, topping their goal-kicking in 1975, but his form deteriorated to the point where he was tried at full-back. An injury during the 1977 season to a ruckman saved Teasdale's place in the senior team, for he was moved into the ruck to replace the injured follower because he was the tallest person for the job, according to coach Ian Stewart. Teasdale was an instant success, with his mobility and athleticism dominating the competition to such an extent that on Brownlow medal night he was awarded the game's highest individual honour, polling 59 votes to beat former Richmond teammate, Kevin Bartlett, 45 votes.*

*   *I wish they had left him at full-back!*

• • •

Since the League started asking players to the Brownlow medal count in 1970, it has never been embarrassed by the winner not being invited. But folklore has it that in 1971, only the second year of players being in attendance, a shudder went through the top table. General manager Jack Hamilton was calling out the votes, which were handed to him by one of his two ICs, Alan Schwab. A bolter, Fitzroy ruckman Alex Ruscuklic, shot to the front with 16 votes, which led Schwabb to mention to Hamilton that Ruscuklic was not an invited guest, and an embarrassing moment could be near. The jokester Hamilton was reported as saying, 'As long as I'm calling the votes, he'll never win.' As it turned out, Ruscuklic didn't poll another vote, and the medal was won by Richmond's Ian Stewart for the third time with 21 votes.

• • •

Only four players in the history of the game have kicked more than 140 goals in a League season. Yet not one of them was able to win the Brownlow medal. Bob Pratt booted 150 goals in 1934, and polled 13 votes, to finish eighth in the count. In 1970, Peter Hudson and Peter McKenna kicked 146 and 143 goals respectively without winning. Hudson, finishing eighth, and McKenna eleventh, with 14 and 10 votes. In 1971, Hudson equalled Pratt's all-time record with 150 goals, but had to be content with second. And in 1992, Jason Dunstall, with 142 goals, was runner-up with eighteen votes to Footscray's Scott Wynd. But spare a thought for North Melbourne's Doug Wade, who reached 103 goals in 1974, and failed to poll a vote in the Brownlow medal.

• • •

Carlton's Greg Williams is on record as saying he knew he wasn't going to win the 1993 Brownlow medal after the votes for Round 10 were announced. The

Blues' centreman was a warm favourite to win his second medal and in Round 10 was voted best on ground by all sections of the media for his superlative performance against Melbourne at Princes Park. Williams amassed over 40 possessions to mesmerize the Demons and set up Carlton's 54-point victory. But to the surprise of the hushed boardroom, Williams failed not only to get the three votes for the best on ground, but failed to gain a vote from the men in white. At the count's end, Williams had lost the game's highest individual honour by one vote to Essendon's Gavin Wanganeen.

The History of the Brownlow Medal

The Charles Brownlow Medal was first awarded in 1924 to the best and fairest player in the home and away series. It was named after Charles Brownlow, an administrator from the Geelong Football Club, who died in that year.

From 1924 to 1930 the medal was decided by the votes of the field umpire, who awarded one vote to the best player in each game. Since 1931, the umpire has awarded three votes to the best player, two to the second best and one to the third best. (In 1976 and 1977, twelve votes were awarded — six from each umpire.)

In 1980 it was decided that players with equal votes should both receive a medal. Previously there had been a countback system — a player with 16 votes made up of four 3s and two 2s defeated a player with 16 votes made up of three 3s, three 2s and a 1. In 1989, retrospective medals were awarded to past players beaten on a countback.

Since 1991, umpires have awarded votes regardless of whether a player is reported. Players found guilty — except those found guilty of a striking charge — are subsequently ruled ineligible.

• Quick Quiz •

1   Who was the first player to win two Brownlow medals?

2   In which season did Bob Skilton win his first Brownlow medal?

3   How many club best and fairest awards did Michael Tuck win?

4   Name the two League players who each won an incredible nine club best and fairest awards.

5   Who was awarded the 1982 Norm Smith medal?

6   Since 3–2–1 voting for the Brownlow medal was introduced, who has won with the smallest number of votes?

7   Name the North Melbourne player who won the Brownlow medal retrospectively.

8   Who won the first Brownlow medal with both field umpires casting votes on a 3–2–1 basis.

9   Name the Brownlow medallist who had the nickname 'Chicken'.

10   Name the players who have won the Brownlow medal in their first season of League football.

Answers

1   Ivor Warne-Smith (Melbourne).

2   1959.

3   None.

4   Bob Skilton (South Melbourne) and Kevin Murray (Fitzroy).

5   Maurice Rioli (Richmond).

6   Greg Williams (1986, Sydney) and Robert DiPierdomenico (1986, Hawthorn).

7   Noel Teasdale, 1965.

8   Graham Moss (1976 Essendon).

9   Wilfred 'Chicken' Smallhorn.

10   Haydn Bunton (1931, Fitzroy) and Brad Hardie (1985, Footscray).

BROWNLOW MEDAL WINNERS 1924–1994

Year	Winner	Club	Votes	Age	No.	Position
1924	Greeves, E 'Carji'	Geelong	7	20	20	centreman
1925	Watson, Colin	St Kilda	9	24	31	wing/centre
1926	Warne-Smith, Ivor	Melbourne	9	28	14	foll/centre
1927	Coventry, Syd	Collingwood	7	28	7	foll/def
1928	Warne-Smith, Ivor	Melbourne	8	30	14	foll/centre
1929	Collier, Albert	Collingwood	6	20	5	half-back
1930	Judkins, Stan	Richmond	4	22	6	winger
	Hopkins, Allan	Footscray	4	26	1	centre
	Collier, Harry	Collingwood	4	22	7	rover
1931	Bunton, Haydn	Fitzroy	26	20	7	rover
1932	Bunton, Haydn	Fitzroy	23	21	7	rover
1933	Smallhorn, W 'Chicken'	Fitzroy	18	22	21	winger
1934	Reynolds, Dick	Essendon	19	19	3	rover
1935	Bunton, Haydn	Fitzroy	24	24	7	rover
1936	Ryan, Dinny	Fitzroy	26	19	4	half-back
1937	Reynolds, Dick	Essendon	27	22	3	rover
1938	Reynolds, Dick	Essendon	18	23	3	rover
1939	Whelan, Marcus	Collingwood	23	25	28	centreman
1940	Fothergill, Des	Collingwood	32	20	6	rover
	Matthews, Herbie	South Melbourne	32	24	1	centreman
1941	Ware, Norman	Footscray	23	30	4	follower
Award suspended during WW2 — 1942–1945						
1946	Cordner, Don	Melbourne	20	24	21	follower
1947	Deacon, Bert	Carlton	20	23	23	half-back
1948	Morris, W (Bill)	Richmond	24	26	5	follower
1949	Clegg, Ron	South Melbourne	23	21	23	half-back
	Austen, Col	Hawthorn	23	28	9	half-back
1950	Ruthven, Alan	Fitzroy	21	27	7	rover
1951	Smith, Bernie	Geelong	23	21	11	back pocket
1952	Wright, Roy	Richmond	21	23	2	follower
	Hutchison, Bill	Essendon	21	29	7	rover
1953	Hutchison, Bill	Essendon	26	30	7	rover
1954	Wright, Roy	Richmond	29	25	2	follower
1955	Goldsmith, Fred	South Melbourne	21	23	2	full-back
1956	Box, Peter	Footscray	22	24	5	centreman
1957	Gleeson, Brian	St Kilda	24	22	30	follower
1958	Roberts, Neil	St Kilda	20	25	10	half-back
1959	Skilton, Bob	South Melbourne	20	20	14	rover
	Howell, Verdun	St Kilda	20	21	16	full-back
1960	Schultz, John	Footscray	20	21	14	follower
1961	James, John	Carlton	21	27	10	half-back
1962	Lord, Alistair	Geelong	28	22	4	centreman
1963	Skilton, Bob	South Melbourne	20	24	14	rover
1964	Collis, Gordon	Carlton	27	23	17	half-back
1965	Stewart, Ian	St Kilda	20	22	5	centreman

BROWNLOW MEDAL WINNERS 1924–1994 (cont).

	Teasdale, Noel	North Melbourne	20	27	2	ruckman
1966	Stewart, Ian	St Kilda	21	23	5	centreman
1967	Smith, Ross	St Kilda	24	24	3	rover
1968	Skilton, Bob	South Melbourne	24	29	14	rover
1969	Murray, Kevin	Fitzroy	19	31	1	ruck/rover
1970	Bedford, Peter	South Melbourne	25	23	11	rover/centre
1971	Stewart, Ian	Richmond	21	28	2	centreman
1972	Thompson, Len	Collingwood	25	25	3	ruckman
1973	Greig, Keith	North Melbourne	27	21	27	winger
1974	Greig, Keith	North Melbourne	27	22	27	winger
1975	Dempsey, Gary	Footscray	20	26	24	ruckman
1976	Moss, Graham	Essendon	48	26	25	ruckman
1977	Teasdale, Graham	South Melbourne	59	22	20	ruckman
1978	Blight, Malcolm	North Melbourne	22	28	15	ruck/rover
1979	Moore, Peter	Collingwood	22	22	30	ruckman
1980	Templeton, Kelvin	Footscray	23	23	31	centre half-forward
1981	Quinlan, Bernie	Fitzroy	22	30	5	ruck/rover
	Round, Barry	South Melbourne	22	31	25	ruckman
1982	Wilson, Brian	Melbourne	23	20	7	centre
1983	Glendinning, Ross	North Melbourne	24	27	4	centre half-back
1984	Moore, Peter	Melbourne	24	27	30	ruckman
1985	Hardie, Brad	Footscray	22	22	4	back-pocket
1986	DiPierdomenico, Robert	Hawthorn	17	28	9	winger
	Williams, Greg	Sydney	17	22	2	centre
1987	Lockett, Tony	St Kilda	20	21	14	full-forward
	Platten, John	Hawthorn	20	24	44	rover
1988	Healy, Gerard	Sydney	20	28	3	ruck/rover
1989	Couch, Paul	Geelong	22	25	7	centre
1990	Liberatore, Tony	Footscray	18	24	39	rover
1991	Stynes, Jim	Melbourne	25	25	11	ruckman
1992	Wynd, Scott	Footscray	20	22	15	ruckman
1993	Wanganeen, Gavin	Essendon	18	20	4	back-pocket
1994	Williams, Greg	Carlton	30	30	2	centre

THE BROWNLOW MEDAL VOTING

1924-30	One vote per match by field umpire.
1931-75	Three-two-one votes per match by field umpire.
1976-77	Three-two-one votes (total of 12) by each of the two field umpires.
1978-	Three-two-one votes (total of 6) by the two field umpires after conferring.

Most AFL Matches by A Brownlow Medallist:
Bernie Quinlan 366 (club matches only)
Most AFL Goals by a Brownlow Medallists:
Tony Lockett 898

EQUAL TOP VOTES

1924-80 Count-back system. Player with the most threes/twos declared the winner.
1981– No count-back system. More than one winner possible.
1989 Previous loses on count-backs awarded Brownlow Medal retrospectively.

PRESENTATION

1924–32 Votes counted at VFL meeting at Harrison House early in the week following the last home-and-away round. Winner notified by mail and asked to collect medal from VFL Headquarters.
1933 Medal presented to the winner at the MCG on First Semi-Final day.
1970 First Channel Seven telecast of the count. Medal presented that night.
1978 Medal count changed to Grand Final Week.
1984 Votes revealed match-by-match.

INELIGIBLE PLAYERS

1924-88 Players who were reported, found guilty and suspended during that season.
1979 Players reported and suspended in a final became eligible.
1989 Players who were reported in a match where Brownlow Medal votes were cast, and found guilty, irrespective of penalty.
  Exception: Players found guilty of a time-wasting charge.

100 OR MORE BROWNLOW VOTES IN A CAREER 1924–94

Name	Clubs		Career Votes	Adjusted Career Votes#
Dempsey, Gary	Footscray	1967-78; 1979-84	246	218.5
Matthews, Leigh	Hawthorn	1969-85	202	173.5
Skilton, Bob	South Melbourne	1956-68; 1970-71	180	
Murray, Kevin	Fitzroy	1955-64; 1967-74	178	
Hutchison, Bill	Essendon	1942-57	172	
Wilson, Garry	Fitzroy	1971-84	161	138.5
Bartlett, Kevin	Richmond	1965-83	160	136.5
Reynolds, Dick	Essendon	1933-51	154	
Thompson, Len	Collingwood	1965-78		
	South Melbourne	1979		
	Fitzroy	1980	151	127
Greig, Keith	North Melbourne	1971-85	151	144
Flower, Robert	Melbourne	1973-87	150	130.5
Stewart, Ian	St Kilda	1963-70		
	Richmond	1971-75	139	
Madden, Simon	Essendon	1974-92	139	125
Bourke, Francis	Richmond	1967-81	139	

100 OR MORE BROWLOW VOTES IN A CAREER (cont.)

Williams, Greg*	Geelong	1984-85		
	Sydney	1986-91		
	Carlton	1992-94	138	
Ware, Norman	Footscray	1932-42; 1944-46	130	
Jesaulenko, Alex	Carlton	1967-79		
	St Kilda	1980-81	129	116.5
Wells, Greg	Melbourne	1969-80		
	Carlton	1980-82	129	106
Quinlan, Bernie	Footscray	1969-77		
	Fitzroy	1978-86	129	119.5
Knights, Peter	Hawthorn	1969-85	126	101
Bunton, Haydn	Fitzroy	1931-37; 1942	122	
Davis, Barry	Essendon	1961-72		
	North Melbourne	1973-75	121	
Cloke, David	Richmond	1974-82; 1990-91		
	Collingwood	1983-89	121	121
Clegg, Ron	South Melbourne	1945-54; 1956-60	120	
Glendinning, Ross	North Melbourne	1978-86		
	West Coast	1987-88	120	
Platten, John*	Hawthorn	1986-94	118	
Matthews, Herbie	South Melbourne	1932-45	116	
Clarke, Jack	Essendon	1951-67	116	
Round, Barry	Footscray	1969-75		
	South Melbourne	1976-85	116	102
Dwyer, Laurie	North Melbourne	1956-58; 1960-64; 1966-70		115
Madden, Justin*	Essendon	1980-82		
	Carlton	1983-94	115	
Whitten, Ted	Footscray	1951-70	112	
Schultz, John	Footscray	1958-68	111	
Moore, Peter	Collingwood	1974-82		
	Melbourne	1983-87	108	101
Dunstall, Jason*	Hawthorn	1985-94	107	
Bray, Harold	St Kilda	1941-43; 1945-52	106	
Nicholls, John	Carlton	1957-74	101	
Smallhorn, W 'Chicken'	Fitzroy	1930-40	100	100
Roos, Paul*	Fitzroy	1982-94	98	

*Denotes current player

#From 1976-77 each field umpire allocated 3-2-1 votes for each match. Players votes have been halved for those seasons to balance aggregates.

BROWNLOW MEDALLISTS WHO COACHED AFL CLUBS

Watson, Colin — St Kilda 1934
Warne-Smith, Ivor — Melbourne 1928-32
Coventry, Syd — Footscray 1936-37
Bunton, Haydn — Fitzroy 1936
Reynolds, Dick — Essendon 1939-60 (Premiers 1942, 1946, 1949, 1950)
Matthews, Herbie — South Melbourne 1939, 1954-57
Ware, Norman — Footscray 1941-42
Clegg, Ron — South Melbourne 1958-59
Ruthven, Alan — Fitzroy 1952-54
Skilton, Bob — South Melbourne 1965-66; Melbourne 1974-77
Stewart, Ian — South Melbourne 1976-77, 1979-81; Carlton 1978 (part)
Smith, Ross — St Kilda 1977
Murray, Kevin — Fitzroy 1963-64
Blight, Malcolm — North Melbourne 1981 (part); Geelong 1989-94
Quinlan, Bernie — Fitzroy 1995

YOUNGEST AND OLDEST BROWNLOW MEDALLISTS
Ages on Monday following the last home-and-away round of the season.
Youngest

'Dinny' Ryan (Fitzroy) 1936	19 years 59 days
Dick Reynolds (Essendon) 1934	19 years 90 days
Des Fothergill (Collingwood) 1940	20 years 49 days
'Leeter' Collier (Collingwood) 1930	20 years 68 days
Haydn Bunton (Fitzroy) 1931	20 years 71 days
Gavin Wanganeen (Essendon) 1993	20 years 96 days
Bob Skilton (South Melbourne) 1959	20 years 296 days
'Carji' Greeves (Geelong) 1924	20 years 312 days
Brian Wilson (Melbourne) 1982	20 years 355 days

Oldest

Barry Round (South Melbourne) 1981	31 years 238 days
Kevin Murray (Fitzroy) 1969	31 years 75 days
Greg Williams (Carlton) 1994	30 years 361 days
Ivor Warne-Smith (Melbourne) 1928	30 years 308 days
Norman Ware (Footscray) 1941	30 years 180 days
Bill Hutchison (Essendon) 1953	30 years 125 days
Bernie Quinlan (Fitzroy) 1981	30 years 62 days

BROWNLOW MEDALLISTS WHO DID NOT PLAY IN A FINAL
Colin Watson — St Kilda 1925
Haydn Bunton — Fitzroy 1931, 1932, 1935
W. 'Chicken' Smallhorn — Fitzroy 1933
'Dinny' Ryan — Fitzroy 1936
Fred Goldsmith — South Melbourne 1955
Brian Gleeson — St Kilda 1957

WINNERS OF FIVE OR MORE CLUB BEST AND FAIREST AWARDS 1897–1994

No.	Player	Club	Years
9	Skilton, Bob	South Melbourne	1958, 1959, 1961, 1962, 1963, 1964, 1965, 1967, 1968
9	Murray, Kevin	Fitzroy	1956, 1958, 1960, 1961, 1962, 1963, 1964, 1968, 1969
8	Matthews, Leigh	Hawthorn	1971, 1972, 1974, 1976, 1977, 1978, 1980, 1982
7	Reynolds, Dick	Essendon	1934, 1936, 1937, 1938, 1939, 1942, 1943
7	Hutchison, Bill	Essendon	1946, 1948, 1950, 1952, 1953, 1955, 1956
7	Dempsey, Gary	Footscray	1970, 1973, 1974, 1975, 1976, 1977
		North Melbourne	1979
6	Murphy, John	Fitzroy	1968, 1970, 1971, 1973, 1977
		South Melbourne	1978
5	Matthews, Herbie	South Melbourne	1936, 1937, 1939, 1940, 1943
5	Whitten, Ted	Footscray	1954, 1957, 1958, 1959, 1961
5	Nicholls, John	Carlton	1959, 1963, 1965, 1966, 1967
5	Schultz, John	Footscray	1960, 1962, 1964, 1965, 1966
5	Thompson, Len	Collingwood	1967, 1968, 1972, 1973, 1977
5	Bartlett, Kevin	Richmond	1967, 1968, 1973, 1974, 1977
5	Davis, Barry	Essendon	1968, 1969, 1971
		North Melbourne	1973, 1975
5	Bedford, Peter	South Melbourne	1969, 1970, 1971, 1973, 1975
5	Wilson, Garry	Fitzroy	1972, 1976, 1978, 1979, 1980
5	Roos, Paul	Fitzroy	1985, 1986, 1991, 1992, 1994

Guilty or Not Guilty?

Reports have always been one of the most contentious items in the history of the game. Players facing the Tribunal often have a sudden loss of memory, and what appeared to be a full-blooded punch during the game may end up being described as a mere glancing blow. Players with cut eyes, broken noses and concussion have been known to swear there was nothing in the reported incident.

It's accepted that an unwritten law exists between players not to 'dob in a mate', and details of incidents can elude the memory bank, making only scratchy recall available. Over the years, the Tribunal has had to sift its way through evidence ranging from fantasy and fiction through to fact in its quest for the truth. Suspensions ranging from one week to a life sentence have been handed down, and such decisions guarantee reports will always be one of the biggest talking points of the game!

Fred's Forgiven

North Melbourne's Fred Rutley will never forget the first day of August 1925 when the Shinboners paid host to Geelong at Arden Street. The game was one of the most violent in history, and Rutley was one of six players reported. He faced the Tribunal on two charges of kicking, was found guilty and received a life suspension. Rutley's suspension was lifted after five years and remarkably Rutley pulled on the North Melbourne guernsey again. It was 28 July 1930, and he had served a sentence of 89 matches.

Not Guilty (I think...)

I'll never forget 15 May 1982, because that was the first and only time I was reported during my career. It was my 369th match after almost 17 years of football, giving me the dubious honour of being the most experienced player ever to make his first appearance as the accused at the League Tribunal. I was reported for striking Geelong's Bruce Nankervis at Kardinia Park by umpire Neville Nash. After the game, Geelong coach Bill Goggin was asked what was his reaction to Bartlett being reported. He replied, 'I think Neville Nash will get two weeks.' I was fortunate that the charge was not sustained after a benevolent Tribunal chairman, Jack Gaffney, found me not guilty, thus enabling me to end my career with a clean sheet.

Clean Sheets

Thirty-one players have achieved the honour of representing one or more AFL clubs in a total of 300 or more matches. Only five of them remain unreported throughout their careers, they being John Rantall (South Melbourne and North Melbourne), Gary Dempsey (Footscray and North Melbourne), Barry Round (Footscray and South Melbourne), Dick Reynolds (Essendon) and Wayne Schimmelbusch (North Melbourne).

Greene's Hiccup

Russell Greene is one player who could consider himself unlucky not to join this select band, for he maintained an unblemished record for more than 15 seasons until he incurred the displeasure of an umpire in his 296th match. Appropriately, he was found not guilty of a striking charge. Russell Greene went on to play eight more games for a career tally of 304 matches.

Opposite page: Tony Lockett, St Kilda, is reported in a match against Sydney in 1994. (John Daniels/Sporting Pix)

Battle of Boot Hill

On 5 July 1974, Essendon played host to Carlton at Windy Hill. The game was later dubbed 'The Battle of Boot Hill'. It brought back memories of the famous 1945 bloodbath grand final (see below). In the second quarter, Dean Hartigan of Essendon, and Craig Davis of Carlton were both knocked unconscious as every player joined in an ugly brawl. Eight players were reported from each side: for Carlton, Rod Austin, David McKay, Rod Ashman, and Phillip Pinnell (twice) were all booked on striking charges. For Essendon, Ron Andrews, Robin Close, Neville Fields and Laurie Moloney were nabbed for striking and charging by umpire Ian Robinson. Incidentally, Carlton booted 14 goals 1 in that spiteful second quarter and won the match easily by 79 points.

The Blood Bath

The 1945 Grand Final between Carlton and South Melbourne is the most infamous grand final in the history of the game. Ten players were reported and South's Ted Whitfield was suspended for the whole of the 1946 season for being involved in numerous incidents, including pulling his jumper over his head so the umpire couldn't see his number. Jack 'Basher' Williams was outed for eight weeks for adopting a fighting attitude towards the umpire. Carlton strongman Rod McLean also copped four weeks for abusing the goal umpire. Don Grossman, South Melbourne, got eight weeks for striking Jim Moorings of Carlton. Bob Chitty of Carlton got eight weeks for elbowing Bill Williams of South Melbourne. Ron Savage of Carlton got eight weeks for hitting Grossman. Fred Fitzgibbon copped a four week suspension and he wasn't even playing in the game. He was nabbed when two police officers grabbed a spectator wearing an overcoat who rushed onto the ground to join the fight. It was Fitzgibbon, who was already serving a three-week suspension following the preliminary final. And Jim Cleary of South Melbourne, known as 'Gentleman Jim', also received eight weeks for striking Ken Hands.

White Line Fever

Richmond toughman Ricky McLean, whose father had received four weeks after playing for Carlton in the famous 1945 Grand Final against South Melbourne, also finished his league career with a bang against South Melbourne. McLean, playing in the Reserves for the Tigers, was reported on five charges ranging from kicking Tony Franklin to striking Franklin and teammate Bob Beecroft. This was after legend has it he decked about five other players. McLean's coach that day was former Richmond star Barry Richardson, whose vivid memory of the game was hearing McLean shout to the Swans players, 'I'll take you all on in the carpark after the game.'

Richardson's close friend and former Richmond premiership player Gareth Andrews decided to defend McLean. Andrews had never been a Tribunal advocate before. McLean was suspended for 16 weeks after the Tribunal took only 11 minutes to deliberate on the evidence. Andrews must have received life, for he never again represented a reported player.

Cheated of his Glory

If video evidence had have been admissable in 1967, Neville Crowe would have been a Richmond premiership player. Crowe was rubbed out for four weeks for striking Carlton legend John Nicholls in the second semi-final. Nicholls went down after it appeared Crowe had struck him. Crowe pleaded his innocence, and his record showed he had never been reported in his 150-game career. Later, video footage would show Crowe clearly didn't make contact with Nicholls, who went to the ground as if hit to win a free kick. Crowe never again played League football, announcing his retirement before the 1968 season.

The Coleman Crisis

Bomber supporters still claim the 1951 premiership was stolen from them when the Tribunal rubbed out champion full-forward John Coleman. He had been a sensation from his first League game against Hawthorn when he kicked twelve goals. The high-flying Coleman kicked 100 goals in 1949, and 120 goals in 1950, in back-to-back Bomber premierships. But during the first semi-final in 1950, Carlton full-back Harry Caspar struck Coleman, who then retaliated. Both players were reported. Despite not being the instigator of the altercation, Coleman, who kicked seven goals in the match, was rubbed out for four weeks, the same penalty handed down to Caspar. Coleman was distraught, and cried on the steps of Harrison House, the then headquarters of the VFL. Essendon lost the grand final to Geelong by only 11 points.

Big Carl's Diary

St Kilda enforcer and later Melbourne captain and coach Carl Ditterich has a Tribunal record as long as your arm. Ditterich was charged 19 times, being found guilty on 11 occasions, and suspended for a total of 30 weeks. Ditterich was reported for striking Kevin Morris in his last game of football playing for Melbourne against Collingwood, but a benevolent Tribunal chairman Jack Gaffney allowed 'Big Carl' to bow out gracefully. Unfortunately for Big Carl, who was a star from his opening VFL game in 1963, he missed out on the biggest prize of all: St Kilda's only premiership win in its history in

1966. During the second last home and away game of that year, Ditterich was reported for striking Fitzroy wingman Daryl Peoples, and was rubbed out for six weeks. Ditterich retired after 285 games, and two losing St Kilda grand final sides, in 1965 and 1971.

Candid Camera

The League introduced trial by video in 1986. The initiative was forced upon the VFL after legal charges were laid against Hawthorn champion Leigh Matthews for striking Geelong wingman and rover Neville Bruns behind the play in a brawling match at Princes Park in 1985. Matthews wasn't reported by the umpires, but the incident was captured on television. The League, in an attempt to safeguard itself from criticism, initiated the power to report a player on video evidence. A game between Essendon and Sydney in June 1986 saw the first players cited on a video charge. The charges ranged from eye gouging to conduct unbecoming. Four players were charged, with two of them being rubbed out. Essendon's Bryan Wood copped a four-week suspension, as did Sydney's David Bolten. Rod Carter of the Swans was severely reprimanded, and Essendon's Trevor Spencer was found not guilty.

George's Folly

Ian George of St Kilda only played seven games and kicked four goals, but he is part of League history. George was reported in 1973 in a match against Melbourne, and he called video evidence to support his case. In doing so, he became the first player allowed to present footage of a reportable incident as evidence. Unfortunately for George, he was suspended.

He Said...He Said...

The Ken Boyd/John Nicholls incident in 1961 still remains a controversial one. Boyd, the tough South Melbourne ruckman, and Nicholls, the hero of Carlton, clashed strongly during the game but no reports were made. That night on television, Nicholls gave his account of the incident, Then Boyd in a newspaper article told how Nicholls had threatened him during the game, and from a boundary throw-in alleged Nicholls drove his boots into his stomach. Boyd then said he was in agony, so he went up and hit Nicholls as hard

Opposite page: Gary Ayres of Hawthorn and Wayne Weidemann of Adelaide make a point during a match between Adelaide and Hawthorn in 1993 — and were sure to have attracted the umpire's attention! (Tony Feder/Sporting Pix)

as he could. The VFL decided to take action against Boyd, and subsequently rubbed out the Swans big man for twelve weeks. The suspension ended Boyd's VFL career.

Gotcha!

An incident in 1992 involving Geelong star Mark Bairstow and West Coast Eagles big man Glen Jakovich was given the all clear after League watchdogs had viewed a tape of the match. The persistent outcry and screening of the incident on Perth television showing Bairstow colliding with Jakovich as he disposed of the ball pressured the League to re-open the incident. The second time around, Bairstow wasn't so lucky, and was given a two-week suspension, the one and only time a player was charged on trial by video after the all clear for the game was given.

An All-out Brawl

The brawl at Windy Hill in 1974 between Essendon and Richmond is regarded as one of the most spiteful games in League history. At the time, it was likened to the 1945 bloodbath grand final between Carlton and South Melbourne. It all started just before half-time when Mal Brown of Richmond clashed with Graeme 'Jerker' Jenkins, the ex-Collingwood player now playing for Essendon. As Brown was walking off the ground at half-time, John Cassin of Essendon, who was 19th man and had been sitting on the bench during in the first half, and Bombers runner Laurie Ashley clashed with Brown. As Brown, Cassin and Ashley became embroiled in proceedings, spot fights broke out as other players got involved. It then grew nasty as officials and club personnel and police invaded the ground. The aftermath saw Essendon fitness adviser Jim Bradley, who had run onto the ground, knocked out in a confrontation with Richmond's team manager Graeme Richmond. At the Tribunal hearing, chairman John Winneke found Essendon runner Laurie Ashley guilty of abusive language and suspended him for six matches. Jim Bradley was given a six match penalty for assaulting Mal Brown. John Cassin had an assault charge against Mal Brown not sustained. Ron Andrews was given six matches for assaulting Brian 'The Whale' Roberts. Steven Parsons of Richmond was suspended for four weeks for assaulting Bradley. Mal Brown, reported for hitting runner Ashley, was outed for one week. Richmond team manager Graeme Richmond, in a separate investigation by the League, was fined $2000.

Fabulous Phil Takes a Break

Phil Carman made headlines wherever he played. The enigmatic Carman was the star for Collingwood before crossing to Melbourne, then Essendon, and finally North Melbourne. Former Collingwood coach Tom Hafey believes an indiscretion by Carman cost Collingwood the 1977 premiership. Carman was booked for striking Hawthorn's Michael Tuck in the 1977 Second Semi-final. Carman was outed for two weeks, missing Collingwood's drawn grand final against North Melbourne and the replay the following week. But it was at Essendon that Carman again made headlines after one year with Melbourne. It was Round 5, 1980, and Carman was reported for striking St Kilda big man Garry Sidebottom by boundary umpire Graham Carbery and field umpire John Morgan. In a heated discussion with Carbery, Carman was reported for headbutting the boundary umpire. Carman received sixteen weeks for the headbutting incident, and four weeks for striking Sidebottom. Carman returned in 1981, and was reported in the opening game of the season.

No Case to Answer

Smart thinking by Carlton president George Harris had charges against two Carlton players and two Collingwood players thrown out by the Tribunal. Carlton met Collingwood in Round 4 in 1969 at Princes Park and the game was a tough knock-'em-down affair. Four players, Carlton's Peter Jones and Ricky McLean, along with Collingwood's Len Thompson and Ted Potter, faced striking charges. Harris noted that the umpires had not written out their report sheets and presented them to the clubs in the given time after the game, as specified by the VFL. Harris noted the umpires were about five minutes late in delivering the bad news. The Carlton president raised the matter at the Tribunal, and on a technicality all cases were dismissed.

Following page: An all-out fight breaks out between Collingwood and West Coast players in Round 13 of the 1993 season. (Tony Feder/Sporting Pix)

• Quick Quiz •

1 Which player holds the record for facing the League Tribunal on the most occasions?

2 How many times was North Melbourne's Brownlow medallist Keith Greig reported?

3 Who was reported 18 times during his 18-season League career?

4 Who was the first West Coast player to face the League Tribunal?

5 In which season were players first reported as the result of video investigation?

6 Geelong great Graham 'Polly' Farmer was reported only once in his League career. Who did he allegedly hit in 1966?

7 Melbourne legend Ron Barassi missed playing the 1963 finals series after being found guilty of striking whom?

8 Name the player in 1992 who was found guilty and given a two-match sentence, which was never served.

9 Who missed the 1967 Grand Final after being reported for the first time in 151 games, and never played again?

10 Carl Ditterich missed St Kilda's only premiership victory after being suspended in 1966 for striking which Fitzroy player?

Answers

1 *David Rhys-Jones (South Melbourne/Sydney/Carlton).*

2 *Once.*

3 *Carl Ditterich (St Kilda/Melbourne).*

4 *Alex Ishchenko.*

5 *1986.*

6 *'Delicate' Des Dickson (Hawthorn).*

7 *Roger Dean (Richmond).*

8 *Barry Mitchell (Sydney).*

9 *Neville Crowe, Richmond.*

10 *Daryl Peoples.*

REPORTED PLAYERS 1897–1994

Player	Club	Number of Charges	Times Guilty	Total Matches
Ablett, Gary	Hawthorn Geelong	10	6	13
Andrews, Ron	Essendon	9	7	24
Bews, Andrew	Geelong	7	5	9
Boyd, Ken	Sth Melbourne	7	7	30
Brereton, Dermott	Hawthorn Sydney	16	8	37
Bryce, Ted	Essendon	2	2	23
Burns, Greg	St Kilda	11	6	14
Carman, Phil	Collingwood Essendon Nth Melbourne	9	4	24
Cassin, Jack	Essendon	8	3	4
Chitty, Bob	Carlton	7	3	14
Coghlan, Arthur	Geelong	2	2	29
Conlan, Michael	Fitzroy	14	7	14
Crosswell, Brent	Carlton	8	6	17
Daniher, Terry	Sth Melbourne Essendon	3	2	11
DiPierdomenico Robert	Hawthorn	9	5	18
Ditterich, Carl	St Kilda Melbourne	19	11	30
Downs, Tommy	Carlton	2	2	31
Franks, Albert	Sth Melbourne	2	2	18
Fraser, Mopsy	Richmond	6	3	16
Fraser, Doug	Carlton	1	1	99
Gent, William	Sth Melbourne	2	2	27
Grinter, Rod	Melbourne	10	7	31
Hepburn, Stan	St Kilda	1	1	12
Holden, George	Fitzroy	1	1	19
Irwin, Frank	Carlton	1	1	18
Jackson, Mark	Melbourne St Kilda Geelong	11	8	11
Johnson, Mocha	Carlton	1	1	12
Kink, Rene	Collingwood Essendon St Kilda	6	6	18
Krakouer, Jim	Nth Melbourne St Kilda	16	9	27
Laing, Roy	Essendon	2	2	17
Lang, Alex	Carlton	1	1	101
Langdon, Karl	West Coast	9	6	13
LeLievra, Stan	St Kilda	1	1	12

REPORTED PLAYERS 1897–1994 (cont.)

Lee, Mark	Richmond	13	6	19
Lewis, Johnny	Nth Melbourne	2	1	18
	Melbourne			
Lockett, Tony	St Kilda	10	6	21
Maclure, Mark	Carlton	8	3	6
Macpherson, Steve	Footscray	9	3	5
McLean, Rod	Carlton	6	4	29
Merrett, Roger	Essendon	11	5	13
	Brisbane			
Muir, Robert	St Kilda	12	9	22
Pascoe, Bob	Nth Melbourne	3	2	11
	St Kilda			
Read, Jim	St Kilda	1	1	10
Rhys-Jones, David	Sth Melbourne	25	11	22
	Carlton			
Rutley, Fred	Nth Melbourne	1	1	89
Scott, Don	Hawthorn	11	6	11
Shorten, James	Collingwood	1	1	29
Taylor, Brian	Richmond	9	4	7
	Collingwood			
Thomas, Stan	Geelong	3	2	29
Weightman, Dale	Richmond	15	8	19
Whitfield, Ted	Sth Melbourne	7	5	22
Williams, Greg	Geelong	15	9	21
	Sydney			
	Carlton			
Williams, Jack	Sth Melbourne	6	4	27
Winmar, Nicky	St Kilda	7	3	13

Talls, Smalls, Fats, Thins...

Is it possible to play League football if you're a Tom Thumb? Can a praying mantis get a kick? Do you have to be an athlete or can you be a gasometer? Are you allowed to turn up in a school uniform? And age... does it matter?

The fact is, there are no criteria or prototype models that designate who can play the game. Fats, thins, talls, shorts, quick, slows, old and young have all played to great effect, and have left their mark on the history of the game.

Footscray rover Tony Liberatore heads the list as the shortest modern day player. Liberatore stands tall at 164 centimetres. For comparison with some of the game's shortest players, 'Libba' would have towered over former Collingwood and North Melbourne rover James 'Nipper' Bradford, who played in the 1940s. Bradford was only 154 centimetres.

• • •

The youngest player to reach 200 AFL games was Hawthorn's Alan Martello. 'Big Al' was 26 years and two days when he chalked up his milestone in the 1978 Second Semi-final against North Melbourne. Martello booted two goals that day. Martello played only another 56 games, falling well short of the 300-games club, and finished his career at Richmond in 1983.

• • •

Fitzroy caused a sensation in 1967 by naming an unknown kid, Andrew Kuka, in the seniors for its Round 10 clash with Essendon. The Lions decided to name the youngster so they could claim him as their player before the intro-duction of country zoning*. Kuka returned home to Morwell the following week and never again played a senior game. Kuka, at 16 years and 46 days, still remains the youngest ever senior player to wear the Fitzroy colours.

* *In 1968, the VFL introduced country zoning. Each club was given a Victorian country area to develop. Players in that area could only play with the zone club. Before zoning, players could be recruited by any League club. The scheme was abandoned in 1986 with the introduction of the national draft system.*

• • •

One of Carlton's great small men, Jimmy Buckley, has the honour of being the Blues' youngest ever player. Buckley was 16 years and 200 days when he lined up against Footscray in Round 11, 1976. Buckley went on to play 164 games and kick 146 goals, play in three premierships, and win a club best and fairest award (1982) during his 13 seasons at Princes Park.

• • •

Carlton's Jim Flynn holds the record as the oldest player to play in a League final. Flynn had blown out the candles on his 40th birthday cake when he lined up for the Blues against South Melbourne at the MCG in 1910. Flynn had retired two years earlier, but controversial circumstances saw his return. Prior to the game, three Carlton stars were dropped after accusations that they had accepted a bribe to play below their best against South. Flynn offered his services to his old club, and he was snapped up.

• • •

The oldest player to pull on the boots for his debut in League football was Essendon's George Rawle. He was 33 years old when selected by the Bombers for the 1923 Grand Final against Fitzroy, which Essendon won. The following year, he again helped the 'Dons to another flag, this time beating Richmond. Rawle played 19 games and kicked 4 goals during his unique career.

• • •

Richmond's Bill James played one game of League football for one premiership win. James played for Kyabram when Richmond became aware of his abilities. When several of the Tigers' players became unavailable for the 1920 Grand Final, selectors called up James, who scored a goal in the Tigers' win over Collingwood. James never played another League game, for after returning home to Kyabram he lost his toes from one foot in a shooting accident while hunting rabbits.

• • •

Glen Jakovich of the West Coast Eagles has the honour of playing 100 League games faster than anyone else. He achieved this in four years and 22 days, when playing against Geelong in Round 22 of the 1995 season, and in doing so surpassed Wayne Schimmelbusch's (North Melbourne) previous record of four years and 32 days. After Schimmelbusch comes Stephen Kernahan (Carlton) with four years and 35 days, John Platten (Hawthorn), four years and 42 days, Alan Martello (Hawthorn) four years and 87 days, and Brian Wood (Richmond) four years, 87 days.

• • •

It's in the record books as the most one-sided game in League history: St Kilda, playing against Geelong in the last home and away game of 1899, scored the first behind of the match. No-one could have guessed that the Saints' scoring feast had ended. The Cats then piled on 23 goals 24 behinds without St Kilda again troubling the scorer. The Saints' final score of 1 point remains an all-time low. Geelong forward Jim McShane that day booted 11 goals, to become the first player to score double figures in a League game.

• • •

The fans certainly got their money's worth in Round 17, 1983, in the match between Fitzroy and St Kilda at the Junction Oval. In the second quarter, the Lions kicked 12 goals 6 (78 points) to St Kilda's 7 goals 1 (43 points). That second quarter scoring frenzy is the highest aggregate score in any quarter of League football.

• • •

Aubrey McKenzie made his League debut for Melbourne on 8 July 1914 against Essendon at the East Melbourne Cricket Ground. After gaining selection in the last match of that season against South Melbourne at the Lake Oval, he turned his back on the VFL to play with Footscray in the VFA. In 1922, he was persuaded to join St Kilda, where he played the first nine matches of the year. He played his last League match against Fitzroy at the Brunswick Street Oval on 15 July. Remarkably, he had taken almost exactly eight years to accumulate 11 VFL games. In contrast, Melbourne's Jim Stynes played 180 senior matches in his first eight years.

• • •

North Melbourne's fiery utility John Cassin must have thought the 1977 season was never going to end. The Kangaroos experienced a magnificent year, winning their second premiership after first playing a tied grand final then beating Collingwood in the play-off. North's performance was remarkable as the team played five finals in 29 days. Cassin created a record by becoming the only League player to play 27 League games in a season.

• • •

Heavy rain brought on atrocious conditions for the 1927 Grand Final between Collingwood and Richmond, yet 34 551 loyal fans braved the elements to watch the two sides slog it out. An extra highlight was the prediction that Magpie star Gordon Coventry would score five goals to make his 100 in a season — a target never before reached in League history. Coventry remained goalless in the first quarter, but booted two goals in ten minutes during the second term to put the 'Pies in front, to become their only goalkicker for the first half. The conditions became so bad that Collingwood failed to score another goal for the match, and the rain certainly robbed Coventry of the first ever 100-goals in a season. He ended the year on 97 goals, with the Magpies taking the flag with 2 goals 13 (25) points to defeat Richmond, 1 goal 7 (13).

• • •

The first player to reach the 300-game milestone was the great Collingwood full-forward Gordon Coventry, who finished his career with 306 games and 1299 goals. The youngest player to reach the 300-game mark was Essendon's Simon Madden at 30 years, 234 days. Second youngest was former St Kilda/Hawthorn utility Russell Greene, at 31 years and 76 days. And the third youngest to the milestone was Collingwood champion ruckman Len Thompson, who was 31 years 166 days.

• • •

In League history, there has only been one scoreless quarter of football. It took place at the Brunswick Street Oval in 1901 during a clash between Fitzroy and Collingwood. Because of a time-keeping mistake, the last quarter lasted only for twenty minutes, in which time neither side had scored. When the bell went, Fitzroy was 5 points down and had the ball on its forward line. An official appeal was made to the VFL, but it was dismissed.

• • •

Audley Gillespie-Jones played for Melbourne and Fitzroy; Rochford Devenish-Meares played for Hawthorn, as did Robert DiPierdomenico, and they all boasted fourteen letters in their surnames. Fourteen letters once gave them the longest surnames to play the game until an Aboriginal player, Che Cocka-too-Collins, made his debut for Essendon in 1994. With 15 letters in his name, he now stands alone as the player with the longest surname in League history.

• • •

The Geelong players certainly had the right boot polish on when they took on St Kilda in Round 5 in 1979 at Moorabbin. The Cats had previously enjoyed little success at the ground, but between the eight-minute mark of the second quarter and the 22nd minute mark of the last quarter, the Cats booted 15 goals straight — a League record for scoring the most consecutive goals without a behind. Geelong won the match 22 goals 10 (142) to St Kilda's 17 goals 10 (112).

• • •

The record for the most behinds in a League match was scored at the MCG in 1974 when a total of 51 behinds was scored by Richmond and South Melbourne. Final scores: Richmond, 23 goals 24 (162) defeated South Melbourne 17 goals 27 (129). Twenty-three players scored minus scores, with the chief offenders being John Pitura, who booted 3 goals 7 behinds, and Kevin Bartlett, who booted 1 goal 7 for Richmond. (Pathetic!)

Opposite page: Justin Madden (left) and Fraser Murphy, a tall and a short player from Carlton. (Sporting Pix)

• • •

There was once conjecture as to who was the tallest player to play League football. It was then agreed that Justin Madden (Essendon/Carlton), Paul Salmon (Essendon), Dean Farnham (Fitzroy) and Ty Esler (Richmond), all standing at 206 centimetres, jointly held the tallest tag. But that was all changed when Matthew Burton made his debut for Fremantle against Richmond in the opening game of the 1995 season. At 210 centimetres, the 'Spider' is the undisputed King of the Tape!

• • •

North Melbourne ruckman Mick Nolan wasn't nicknamed the 'Galloping Gasometer' after the famous North Melbourne landmark for nothing*. Nolan is on record as the heaviest League player. He tipped the scales at 124 kilograms and was a member of North's first-ever premiership team in 1975. Nolan has an eight-kilogram weight advantage over his nearest rival, Richard Lounder (who played four games for Richmond in 1989), with another kilo to Dean Farnham of Fitzroy (1974–75). Brian 'The Whale' Roberts (who played for Richmond and South Melbourne in the years 1971–75), at a miserly, minnow-size of 113 kg, is a distant fourth

* *The Gasworks Gasometer formerly overlooked the North Melbourne home ground at Arden Street.*

• • •

Light as a feather just about describes George Shorten, who played 53 games for Essendon between 1923 and 1926. Shorten was truly jockey-sized, and that 47 kilograms makes him the lightest player ever to play League football. Renowned lightweight Kevin 'Skeeter' Coghlan (playing for Collingwood and Hawthorn and a member of the famous Channel 7 'World of Sport' panel) weighed in at a *massive* 55 kilograms. Lightest of the present day players is former St Kilda rover, now Brisbane Bear, Danny Craven, who tips the scales at 66 kilograms.

• Quick Quiz •

1   Who is the tallest player to gain selection in 250 League matches?

2   How old was Vic Cumberland when he played his last match for St Kilda in 1920?

3   Who was the youngest ever League player?

4   Name the shortest League player to gain selection in the 1995 season.

5   Who was the heaviest player selected in the 1966 Grand Final?

6   Name the youngest player to play for Adelaide.

7   Name the youngest player to play for Richmond.

8   Name the youngest player to play for Melbourne.

9   Name the youngest player to play for West Coast.

10   Name the youngest player to play for North Melbourne.

Answers

1   *Justin Madden (Essendon/Carlton).*

2   *43 years of age.*

3   *Keith Bromage. He was 15 years and 287 days when he first played for Collingwood.*

4   *Danny Craven, of Brisbane.*

5   *Ray Gabelich of Collingwood.*

6   *Ben Hart (17 years, 257 days).*

7   *Mick Maguire (15 years, 328 days).*

8   *Sid Catlin (16 years, 230 days).*

9   *Chris Lewis (18 years, 159 days).*

10   *Rob Peterson (16 years, 45 days).*

HEAVIEST PLAYERS 1897–1994

Name	Club	Career Span	Weight
Nolan, Mick	North Melbourne	1973-80	124
Lounder, Richard	Richmond	1989	116
Farnham, Dean	Fitzroy	1974-75	115
Roberts, Brian	Richmond	1971-75	113
	South Melbourne	1975	
Salmon, Paul*	Essendon	1983-94	112
Ishchenko, Alex*	West Coast	1987-88	110
	Brisbane	1989-91	
	North Melbourne	1992-94	
Moffatt, Hugh	Richmond	1921-22	110
Cloke, David	Richmond	1974-92	110
Rocca, Saverio*	Collingwood	1992-94	107
Gabelich, Ray	Collingwood	1955-60	106
		1962-66	
Dear, Paul*	Hawthorn	1987;1989-94	105
Round, Barry	Footscray	1969-75	105
	South Melbourne	1976-85	
Wynd, Scott*	Footscray	1988-94	105
Esler, Ty	Richmond	1991-93	104
Monkhorst, Damian*	Collingwood	1988-94	104
Neale, Kevin	St Kilda	1965-77	104
Negri, Romano	Adelaide	1991	104
Spalding, Earl*	Melbourne	1987-91	104
	Carlton	1992-94	
Thompson, Len	Collingwood	1965-78	104
	South Melbourne	1979	
	Fitzroy	1980	
Ironmonger, John	Sydney	1985-87	102
	Fitzroy	1988;1990-91	
Lockett, Tony*	St Kilda	1983-94	102
Loewe, Stewart*	St Kilda	1986-94	102
Longmire, John*	North Melbourne	1988-94	102
Madden, Justin*	Essendon	1980-82	101
	Carlton	1983-94	
Dempsey, Gary	Footscray	1967-78	100
	North Melbourne	1979-84	
Ditterich, Carl	St Kilda	1963-72	100
		1976-78	
	Melbourne	1973-75	
		1979-80	
Martello, Alan	Hawthorn	1970-80	100
	Richmond	1981-83	
Martyn, Michael*	Nth Melbourne	1988-94	100

* *Denotes current player*

LIGHTEST PLAYERS 1897–1994

Name	Club	Career Span	Weight
Shorten, George	Essendon	1923-26	47
Bradford, James	Collingwood	1943	52
	North Melbourne	1949	
Carney, Jack	Geelong	1930-34	54
	Carlton	1936-41	
Hardy, Charlie	Essendon	1921-25	54
Coghlan, Kevin	Collingwood	1949-52	55
	Hawthorn	1953-56	
McMaster-Smith, Bruce	Fitzroy	1960-61	60
	Carlton	1962-64	
	St Kilda	1965	
Watt, Rowley	Essendon	1922-31	61
Bailes, Barcley	Fitzroy	1905-09	65
Craven, Danny*	St Kilda	1989-92	66
	Brisbane	1993-94	
Lappin, Matthew*	St Kilda	1994	66
Hutchison, Bill	Essendon	1942-57	69
Lawson, Jamie	Sydney	1991-94	70
Mitchell, Barry*	Sydney	1984-92	70
	Collingwood	1993	
	Carlton	1994	
Naish, Chris *	Richmond	1990-94	70
Platten, John *	Hawthorn	1986-94	70
Weightman, Dale	Richmond	1987-93	70
Wilson, Garry	Fitzroy	1971-84	70

* Denotes current player

YOUNGEST PLAYERS 1897–1994

Name	Club	Years	Days
Hart, Ben*	Adelaide	17	257
Voss, Michael	Brisbane	17	11
Buckley, Jim	Carlton	16	200
Bromage, Keith	Collingwood	15	287
Watson, Tim	Essendon	15	305
Kuka, Andrew	Fitzroy	16	46
James, Ron	Footscray	16	155
Newland, Ken	Geelong	16	74
Peck, John	Hawthorn	16	255
Catlin, Sid	Melbourne	16	230
Peterson, Rob	North Melbourne	16	45
Maguire, Mick	Richmond	15	328
Eicke, Wells	St Kilda	15	315
Hay, Rob	South Melbourne; Sydney	16	285

* Denotes current player

TALLEST PLAYERS 1897–1994

Name	Club	Career Span	Height
Burton, Matthew	Fremantle	1995	210
Esler, Ty	Richmond	1991-93	206
Farnham, Dean	Fitzroy	1974-75	206
Madden, Justin*	Essendon	1980-82	106
	Carlton	1983-94	
Salmon, Paul*	Essendon	1983-94	206
Mustey, Trevor	Sydney	1982-83	204
Negri, Romano	Adelaide	1991	204
Lounder, Richard	Richmond	1989	203
Monkhorst, Damian*	Collingwood	1988-94	203
Willis, David	Sydney	1988-91	203
Heard, Bob	Collingwood	1970-75	202
	Richmond	1976-79	
Ishchenko, Alex*	West Coast	1987-88	201
	Brisbane	1989-91	
	North Melbourne	1992-94	
Wynd, Scott*	Footscray	1988-94	201
Barling, Tim	Richmond	1984-85	200
	Sydney	1989-90	
Ironmonger, John	Sydney	1985-87	200
	Fitzroy	1988	
		1990-91	
Lawrence, Stephen*	Hawthorn	1988-94	200

* Denotes current player

SHORTEST PLAYERS 1897–1994

Name	Club	Career Span	Height
Bradford, James	Collingwood	1943	154
	North Melbourne	1949	
Hardy, Charlie	Essendon	1921-25	156
Bailes, Barcley	Fitzroy	1905-09	157
Speakman, William	Essendon	1927-29	157
Horwood, Ray	Richmond	1950-52	157.5
	Collingwood	1952	
Nicholls, Doug	Fitzroy	1932-37	157.5
Downs, Tommy	Carlton	1927-29	159
		1931	
Carney, Jack	Geelong	1930-34	160
	Carlton	1936-41	
Hall, Clarrie	Richmond	1912-22	160
		1924	
Coghlan, Kevin	Collingwood	1949-52	163
	Hawthorn	1953-56	
Watt, Rowley	Essendon	1922-31	163
Liberatore, Tony*	Footscray	1986-94	164

SHORTEST PLAYERS 1897–1994 (cont.)

Craven, Danny*	St Kilda	1989-92	165
	Brisbane	1993-94	
McMaster-Smith, Bruce	Fitzroy	1960-61	165
	Carlton	1962-64	
	St Kilda	1965	
Shorten, George	Essendon	1923-26	165
Lawson, Jamie	Sydney	1991-94	168

* *Denotes current player*

Footy Families

Following in your father's footsteps is never an easy assignment when it comes to League football. Some sons have suffered in comparison, while others have exceeded the deeds of their fathers. The football lineage includes grandfathers and grandsons carving out their own niche in football history. It's been common for brothers to play the game, but not so common for identical twins. Fathers and sons have worn the same number, won best and fairest awards and played in premiership teams. To help maintain a family tradition, the League now has in place the father and son rule so clubs can continue the lineage. All it takes for a son to follow in his father's footsteps is for the dad to have played fifty games with the one club.

• • •

A number of sets of brothers have played League football but not too many have been goalscoring machines. Only on two occasions have brothers managed as many as 50 majors in a season. In 1928 Jack Baggott of Richmond scored 61 goals, and nine years later his brother Ron booted 51 for Melbourne. Carlton's Brian Kekovich headed the Blues' list with 59 in 1968 to help his side win the premiership. The next year saw his mercurial brother Sam kick 56 for North Melbourne.

• • •

James Joyce, recruited from Yarraville, made his debut for Footscray against Hawthorn at the Western Oval in Round 1 of 1931. In all, he played 13 matches in his only League season and kicked five goals as a wingman. His son Alan went on to play for Hawthorn, and also coached the Hawks to two flags (in 1988 and 1991), and is now the present coach of Footscray.

• • •

Bomber James Hird is fast becoming one of the game's best young players. He starred in Essendon's 1993 premiership win. His father, Allan, played for Essendon in 1966 and '67, and grandfather Allan snr played in Essendon's 1942 premiership side, as well as playing for Hawthorn and St Kilda.

• • •

Hawthorn centre half-forward Jason Taylor is now making a name for himself after starting his career at Fitzroy. His father, Noel, donned the Hawthorn guernsey for his only League game in 1965. Jason's grandfather, Cliff 'Beau' Taylor in 1938 played ten games for Geelong.

• • •

Only on two occasions have fathers and sons kicked 50 goals in a season of League football. South Melbourne's Austin Robertson kicked 53 goals in 1929; his son, Austin jnr, 54 years later, scored 60 goals for the Swans in his only League season in 1966. And Hawthorn's Peter Hudson on six occasions kicked 50 goals or more in a season between 1967 and 1977. His son Paul shot 62 goals for the Hawks in 1991.

Following page: Paul Hudson and father Peter hold the premiership cup after Hawthorn's 1991 Grand Final victory.(Tony Feder/Sporting Pix)

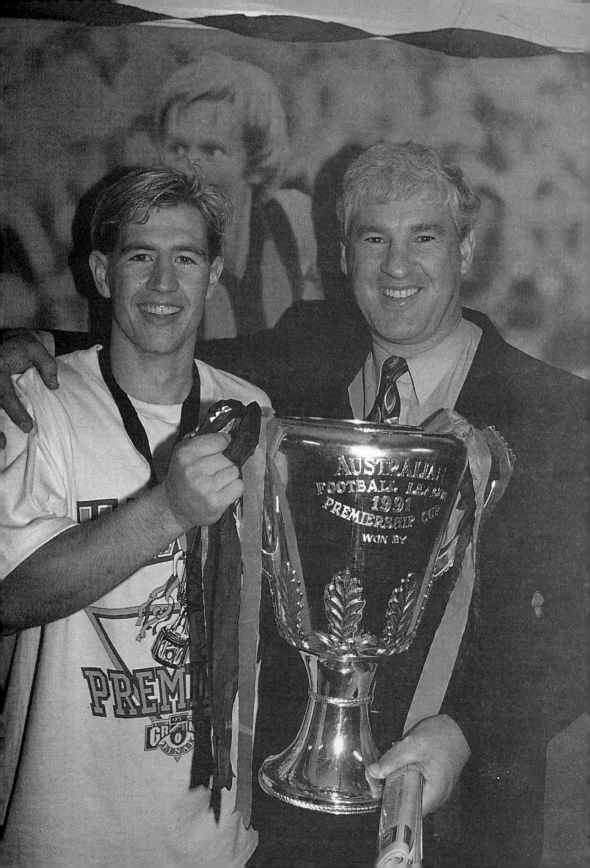

• • •

Gordon Coventry had a day out in Round 12 of 1930 when he booted 17 goals for Collingwood against Fitzroy at Victoria Park. That day, his brother and captain, Sid, kicked one goal. No other set of brothers has contributed as many as 18 goals in one League game.

• • •

The Morwood brothers share a unique League record. The three brothers, Paul, Tony and Shane, all played 100 or more League games. In total, the brothers chalked up 610 games and 594 goals in 17 seasons from 1977 to 1993. Tony played 229 games and kicked 397 goals for South Melbourne and Sydney. Shane played 211 games and kicked 119 goals for South Melbourne, Sydney and Collingwood. Paul played 170 games and kicked 78 goals for South Melbourne, Sydney, St Kilda and Collingwood.

• • •

Graham Cooper was a tough defender and played in Hawthorn's 1961 premiership team. His brother, Ian, five years later, starred in St Kilda's 1-point premiership victory over Collingwood in 1966. Both have the distinction of being members of their clubs' first-ever premiership sides.

• • •

In only one father-son combination has each scored more than 200 career goals. Bob Johnson snr booted 302 goals in his 113-match career with Melbourne from 1926 to 1933. Bob jnr played 140 games for his 267 goals in his eight-year stint with Melbourne, starting in 1954. Both father and son were natural left-footers.

• • •

Two top wingmen of the 1960s, Russell Blew of Essendon and Mick Gaudion of North Melbourne, shared an unusual family connection. For at the same time, their brothers Don Blew and Barry Gaudion were League field umpires.

• • •

Playing for Hawthorn, Leo Murphy won two best and fairest awards between 1930 and 1940. Nearly 30 years later, his son John started a magnificent League career with Fitzroy. With the Lions, John Murphy won 5 best and fairest awards before joining South Melbourne in 1978 when he again won that club's best and fairest, creating a record eight best and fairest awards for a father and son combination.

Football's famous Daniher brothers, Chris, Terry, Neale and Anthony, in their Essendon guernseys. (Sporting Pix)

• • •

Geoff Moriarty started his career in 1898 as a wingman-come-centreman for Fitzroy before developing into a top defender. He retired in 1907 after 104 games without kicking a goal. His son, Jack, in 1922 started his career with Essendon, but only lasted a year before joining his father's old club. At Fitzroy, son Jack kicked 662 goals in 170 games before retiring in 1933. His goal tally still remains a Fitzroy club record.

• • •

In 1905, Bill 'Sonna' Thomas started his career with South Melbourne before joining Richmond. In all, he played 197 matches, missing out on the 200-game milestone in 1919 after breaking his leg and being forced to retire. Son Len, eight years later, played the first of his 208 League games. He started with South Melbourne before joining Hawthorn in 1939. He played his last season of League football with North Melbourne before being killed in the Second World War. No other father and son combination has come closer to the double century milestone.

• • •

Between 1911 and 1968 three generations of the Green family represented Collingwood. Each member was named Jack. The original Jack played 106 games in eight seasons and had a brief spell with Geelong in 1908. His son played 85 games from 1929 to 1933 before joining Hawthorn for another forty games. Jack number 3 wore the Magpie jumper on 18 occasions between 1967 and 1968. Amazingly, 14 of those games were as a reserve, that being 19th or 20th man.

• • •

Over the past 50 years, on five occasions three or more brothers have played in the same match. Collingwood brothers, Bill, Pat and Mick Twomey played 23 games together in 1952 and 1953. The Moorwood brothers, Tony, Paul and Shane, played 15 games for South Melbourne in 1981 and 1982. Shane also played for Collingwood against his Swan brothers in one match. In Round 21 of 1984, Geoff and Kevin Ablett, playing for Richmond, opposed brother Gary playing for Geelong. Footscray brothers Neil, Graeme and Brian Cordy played three games together in 1985. In 1987, Neil and Graeme, then playing for Sydney, lined up against brother Brian for Footscray. The Daniher brothers, Terry, Anthony, Chris and Neale, created history in Round 22, 1990 when all four were selected to play for Essendon against St Kilda. Between 1988 and 1991, Terry, Anthony and Chris played together for the Bombers on numerous occasions. On one occasion in 1985, Neale and Terry, playing for Essendon, opposed brother Anthony who was then playing for Sydney.

• • •

Only on one occasion have brothers opposed one another as captains in a League final. It took place on 14 September 1912 when Essendon played South Melbourne in a semi final at the MCG. The Dons and Swans were captained respectively by Alan and Vic Belcher. Two weeks later, they met in the grand final, but South Melbourne captain Charlie Ricketts returned from injury to lead his side.

• • •

On three other occasions, brothers have been opposed in finals games. John 'Jiggy' Harris played for Collingwood against brother Don who lined up for Richmond in the 1928 Grand Final. Gerard Healy, Sydney, opposed brother Greg, Melbourne, in the first semi-final in 1987, and more recently Glen Jakovich, West Coast, and brother Allen, Melbourne, lined up on opposing sides in the 1991 First Semi-final at Waverley Park.

• • •

Only five pairs of brothers have captained teams in finals matches: Alan Belcher, Essendon; Vic Belcher, South Melbourne; Bert Rankin, Geelong; Cliff Rankin, Geelong; Wayne Richardson, Collingwood; Max Richardson, Collingwood; Bruce Nankervis, Geelong; Ian Nankervis, Geelong; Ray Shaw, Collingwood; Tony Shaw, Collingwood.

• • •

The Smith brothers are the only pair to coach League teams into finals. Norm Smith guided Melbourne in 23 finals for eight grand final appearances and six premierships, in 1955, '56 and '57, '59, '60 and '64. He also coached South Melbourne to one final in 1970. Brother Len coached Fitzroy to three finals matches between 1958 and 1960. They opposed each other in the second semi-final in 1960, which was won by Melbourne.

• • •

It's rare to have three brothers playing together in a League game, let alone having three brothers appear together in a finals game. The first time was in 1897 when the Geelong trio of Henry, Jim and Joe McShane were selected for the finals of that year. Over 50 years later, the Twomey brothers, Bill, Pat and Mick, ran out together for Collingwood in the 1952 second semi and preliminary finals. In 1953, all three played in Collingwood's premiership win over Geelong. Their father, Bill snr, who also won the Stawell Gift, was a member of the Magpie's 1919 flag-winning combination.

• • •

Collingwood's premiership team of 1953 had a real family flavour for, apart from the three Twomey brothers, the line-up included two other sets of brothers, Bob and Bill Rose, and captain Lou and Ron Richards. And, back in the good old days, the 'Pies had three sets of brothers who played eight finals between 1928 and 1930. Sid and Gordon Coventry, Albert and Harry Collier, and Frank and Len Murphy all played in the glorious premiership wins in 1928, 1929 and 1930.

• • •

The Pannam brothers, Charlie and Alby, together with their descendants, played in a remarkable 62 finals matches for Collingwood. Charlie snr played for the 'Pies in the 1902 and 1903 premiership teams; son Charlie jnr played in the 1917 and 1919 premierships; Alby snr played in the 1907 and 1908 finals series, and son Alby jnr played in the 1935 and 1936 premiership wins. Grandsons of Charlie Pannam, Lou and Ron Richards, played in Collingwood's 1953 flag win. All up, three generations of the family repre- sented Collingwood in 15 grand finals and celebrated seven premierships.

• • •

In the history of the VFL/AFL, there have only been eleven known sets of twins to play League football. The only set to play finals was the Lord twins, who were identical. Alistair and Stewart both played in Geelong's last premiership win in 1963. The eleven sets of twins are as follows:

Alistair and Stewart Lord (both played for Geelong)
Fred and Keith Cook (Geelong/Melbourne)
Ted and George Lockwood (both played for Geelong and Collingwood)
Charles and Wally Naismith (Fitzroy/Fitzroy and Melbourne)
Matthew and Steven Febey (both played for Melbourne)*
Michael and Nigel Kol (Geelong/Geelong and Melbourne)
Simon and Paul Atkins (Footscray and Fitzroy/Sydney)
Shane and Darryl Wakelin (both played for St Kilda)*
Michael and Steven Richardson (Collingwood, Essendon, Brisbane/Essendon)
Bert and Ivor Clay (both played for Fitzroy)
Neville and Robert Stibbard (both played for South Melbourne)
*   *Current players*

• • •

John Kennedy snr coached Hawthorn and North Melbourne to 18 finals appearances. Son, John jnr, played in 19 finals for Hawthorn. Both father and son never coached and played in the same final.

• • •

• Quick Quiz •

1   Name the three Twomey brothers who played for Collingwood.

2   Which brothers captained Geelong during the 1970s?

3   Which father/son combination won the North Melbourne best and fairest award in 1957 and 1989/1993?

4   Name the current Hawthorn player whose father was selected in the 1971 premiership team.

5   Which current Essendon player's grandfather coached St Kilda in 1946–47.

6   Name the player, his son, and his grandson who all played in VFL premiership teams.

7   In the past 50 years, name the two sets of brothers who played in VFL premiership teams at different clubs.

8   What pair of brothers played in opposing teams in the same AFL final in 1991?

9   In the last 30 years, name the player who made his VFL debut only four years after his father retired from League football.

10 Geelong full-back Ben Graham's grandfather played 227 games and kicked 231 goals. Which club did he play for?

Answers

10   South Melbourne (1935–49).

9   Ted Whitten jnr (debuted, 1974); Ted Whitten snr (retired 1970).

8   Glen Jakovich (West Coast) and Allen Jakovich (Melbourne).

7   Graham Cooper (Hawthorn, 1961) and Ian Cooper (St Kilda, 1966).
     Brian Kekovich (Carlton, 1968) and Sam Kekovich (North Melbourne, 1975);
     Scott Howell (Carlton, 1981).

6   Jack Howell jnr (Carlton, 1947),
     Jack Howell snr (South Melbourne, 1918),
     James Hird, grandson of Allan Hird.

5   Paul Hudson.

4   Brian and Michael Martyn.

3   Bruce and Ian Nankervis.

2   Bill, Mick and Pat.

1

FATHER/SON COMBINATIONS WHO HAVE WON LEAGUE CLUB BEST AND FAIREST AWARDS 1897–1993

Sergio Silvagni   Carlton 1962, 1968
Stephen Silvagni   Carlton 1990

Tom Clarke   Essendon 1931
Jack Clarke   Essendon 1958, 1962

Leo Murphy   Hawthorn 1936, 1937
John Murphy   Fitzroy 1968 (shared), 1970, 1971, 1973, 1977
South Melbourne 1978

Brian Martyn   North Melbourne 1957
Michael Martyn   North Melbourne 1989, 1990 (shared)

BROWNLOW MEDALLISTS WHOSE SONS PLAYED LEAGUE FOOTBALL

Syd Coventry – Hugh Coventry
Herbie Matthews Snr – Herbie Matthews Jnr
John James – Michael James
Neil Roberts – Michael Roberts
Marcus Whelan – Shane Whelan

BROWNLOW MEDALLISTS WHOSE FATHERS PLAYED LEAGUE FOOTBALL

Kevin Murray – Dan Murray (Fitzroy)
Don Cordner – Ted Cordner (Melbourne/University)
'Carji' Greeves – Edward Greeves Snr (Geelong)
Scott Wynd – Gary Wynd (Melbourne)

BROWNLOW MEDALLISTS WHOSE BROTHERS PLAYED LEAGUE FOOTBALL

Syd Coventry – Gordon Coventry
Norm Ware – Walter Ware
Albert Collier – Harry Collier*
Brian Gleeson – Terry Gleeson
Dick Reynolds – Tom Reynolds
Don Cordner – Denis Cordner, Ted Cordner, John Cordner
Alistair Lord – Stewart Lord
Jim Stynes – Brian Stynes
Gerard Healy – Greg Healy
John Schultz – Robert Schultz

* Albert and Harry Collier are the only brothers to both win a Brownlow medal.
Albert won in 1929, and Harry was awarded the 1930 medal retrospectively.

Numbers Up!

Guernsey numbers have played an integral part in football since 1912. That was the year the VFL established the football record — and every player came onto the field with a number on his back. Prior to numbers, players were distinguished by style and mannerism, and wore only their club colours.

Before 1912, some clubs experimented with numbers, and players first wore numbers in a finals game in 1911 when Essendon and Carlton clashed in the second semi-final. The Essendon captain of the time, Vin Gardiner, has the honour of being the first premiership captain to wear a number — the Devil's 13. Some clubs like Collingwood once insisted that their captains carried the number one on their backs. Today, a player's number is synonymous with the person and many champions have played their entire careers with only the one guernsey number.

Due to the blood rules, season 1994 saw two incidents where players wore three different numbers during the game. The first occasion took place during Round 22 when St Kilda's Rod Keogh wore numbers 17, 60 and 59 against Sydney at Waverley, and the second in Round 24 when Richmond's Matthew Knights, playing against Geelong, wore guernsey numbers, 33, 29 and 54.

• • •

Champion North Melbourne player Barry Cable played all but one of his 116 games in his famous number 9 jumper. The only time 9 didn't grace his back was in the historic North Melbourne 1975 Grand Final win over Hawthorn. Cable arrived at the ground without his jumper, and had to switch to number 44.

• • •

If you want to kick 100 goals in a League season, try jumper number 10, for 10 is the most frequently-worn number to kick a ton. Those to wear 10 include Bob Pratt, South Melbourne, in 1934 and 1935, Bill Mohr, St Kilda, in 1936, and John Coleman, Essendon, in 1949, 1950 and 1952.

• • •

Hawthorn's Peter Hudson has worn the lowest guernsey number to kick 100 goals in a League season. Hudson wore number 1 when he booted 110 goals in 1977. Sydney's Warwick Capper kicked 103 goals in 1987 wearing jumper number 39. Capper's number is the highest carried by a century goalkicker.

• • •

The highest number worn by a Brownlow medallist is number 44, carried by Hawthorn's John Platten, who won the coveted award in 1987. Guernseys never to win the award from the lowest to the highest number are 8, 12, 13, 18, 19, 22, 26, 29, 32, 33, 34, 35, 36, 37, 38, 40, 41, 42, and 43.

• • •

Guernsey number 7 has won the most number of Brownlow medals. Ten times, lucky 7 has polled the most votes. The winners: Syd Coventry, Collingwood, 1927; Harry Collier, Collingwood, 1930; Haydn Bunton, Fitzroy, 1931, 1932, and 1935; Alan Ruthven, Fitzroy, 1950; Bill Hutchison, Essendon, 1952 and 1953; Brian Wilson, Melbourne, 1982; and Paul Couch, Geelong, 1989.

• • •

The first time guernsey numbers were worn regularly in the VFL was in the 1911 finals series. Prior to that, players were identified by mannerisms and appearance. Players names and numbers were displayed on the MCG score-board for the 1911 Grand Final. The football record began publication in 1912 and listed the numbers of players. The tradition continues today.

• • •

Michael Tuck played a record 426 League matches. Not surprisingly, he has played the most games wearing the same guernsey number, 17, which he wore throughout his career. Three present day players have worn their numbers more than any other player: Doug Hawkins, 339 games in number 7*; Peter Rohde, 158 games in number 41*, and Justin Madden, 296 games in number 44*.

*   *These three players are playing in the current 1995 season. These figures were correct at the time of going to press in June 1995.*

• • •

Guernsey number 6 has collectively scored the most number of goals in League history. Players wearing the half-dozen who have scored more than 250 career goals are Peter McKenna, Collingwood; Michael Moncrieff, Hawthorn; John Dugdale, North Melbourne; Cliff Rankin, Geelong; Jack Moriarty, Fitzroy; Fred Fanning, Melbourne; George Bisset, Footscray; and Arnold Briedis, North Melbourne.

• • •

To play 100 games in League football is a milestone of significance. Three father/son combinations have played a century of games wearing the same number. Wearing number 9, Leo Turner played 130 matches for Geelong between 1947 and 1954. His son, Michael Turner, playing for Geelong from 1974 to 1984 and from 1986 to 1988, wore number 9 in 245 games. Brian Pert, playing for Fitzroy from 1954 to 1965, wore number 3 guernsey in 125 matches, while his son Gary Pert, playing for Fitzroy from 1982 to 1990, wore the same number in 163 matches. Finally, Sergio Silvagni of Carlton wore the number 1 guernsey in 226 matches between 1959 and 1971, while his son Stephen Silvagni, also playing for Carlton, has worn the same guernsey on 174* occasions between 1985 and 1995.

*   *Silvagni is playing in the current 1995 season. This figure was correct at the time of going to press in June 1995.*

Opposite page: Former Collingwood champion, Peter Daicos, holder of the number 35 guernsey. (Tony Feder/Sporting Pix)

• • •

In 1958 the VFL ordered players from Melbourne and Collingwood to wear different numbers in the grand final. The direction came after a newspaper published numbers in opposition to the football record. The only player in the 1958 Grand Final to wear his original number was burly Magpie ruckman Ray Gabelich. Gabelich wore his number 13 guernsey because no other one would fit him. A few number changes were also made for the 1965 Second Semi-final between Collingwood and St Kilda, when once again numbers were published without the League's authorisation.

• • •

It's not often players take the field wearing the same number, so spectators rubbed their eyes during the match between Geelong and North Melbourne at Kardinia Park in 1990. Kangaroo Brett Allison swapped to a sleeveless jumper carrying number 32. By mistake, teammate Shaun Smith was already wearing that number. The error was picked up after a short period of time and Allison was given another jumper.

• • •

Numbers were worn for the first time in League history when Fitzroy defeated Collingwood by 17 points in a promotional game played at the Sydney Cricket Ground in 1903. 20 000 spectators turned up, and to aid those who were foreign to the game, small numbers were worn on jumpers, and printed cards with players' names and numbers were distributed on admission.

• • •

Only four players in League history have reached 100 games wearing the high number 44 — and all are still involved in League football. Justin Madden played 296* games with Essendon and Carlton; Richard Osborne, 231* games with Fitzroy, Sydney and Footscray; John Platten, 208* games with Hawthorn, and Shane Kerrison, 136* games with Collingwood.

*   *These players are all playing in the current 1995 season. These figures were correct at the time of going to press in June 1995.*

Opposite page: One of football's living legends, Ron Barassi, playing for Melbourne in the 1950s. Barassi wore the number 31 guernsey in all of his 254 matches for Carlton and Melbourne except for one occasion, the 1958 Grand Final.

• • •

Collingwood player Andrew Witts has the distinction of wearing the highest number in the history of the game. Witts made his debut in 1985 against Essendon at Victoria Park wearing guernsey number 65.

• • •

The most goals scored by a League player wearing guernsey number 13 is 420 by Collingwood champion Dick Lee. He wore the Devil's number from 1914 until 1922, and also carried 10, 16 and 19 on his back at other stages of his career.

• • •

Jack Regan, Collingwood's great defender, was known as the prince of full-backs. He played 196 games over 17 seasons, starting his career in 1930. Regan has the record for wearing the most number of different guernsey numbers. He had 11 numbers during his illustrious time at Victoria Park. His numbers were: 27, 19, 20, 24, 25, 16, 22, 18, 23, 1, and 2.

• • •

In guernsey numbers ranging from 1 to 49, only 45, 46, and 48 have failed to produce a 100-game player. The closest a player has come was when Michael Ford, who played at Footscray and St Kilda with 45 on his back between 1984 and 1992, ended his career on 98 games.

• • •

Four present day players have scored more goals wearing their guernsey numbers than any previous player. The modern day recordholders are Gary Ablett (Geelong) between 1984 and 1994, 830 goals in guernsey number 5; Jason Dunstall (Hawthorn) between 1985 and 1994, 1011 goals in guernsey number 19; Mick McGuane (Collingwood) between 1987 and 1994, 112 goals in guernsey number 34; Richard Osborne (Fitzroy, Sydney) between 1982 and 1994, 482 goals in guernsey number 44.

• • •

Footy fans at the match between Collingwood and Geelong at the Corio Oval in 1940 had to look twice. Two Magpie players, Alby Pannam and Harry Powell, both were wearing number 22 guernseys. In those days, players travelled to Corio by train, and on the way down Pannam accidently spilt a thermos of tea over his gear. Pannam took the field in Powell's spare jumper.

• Quick Quiz •

1   Which Guernsey number was made famous by Bob Skilton?
2   Who wore guernsey number 5 for Geelong immediately before Gary Ablett?
3   In which season did 39 of the 40 selected grand final players wear guernsey numbers that differed from those used regularly during that season?
4   How many League players have worn guernsey number 44 in 100 matches or more?
5   In which year were guernsey numbers first used for an entire season?
6   What number did Bruce Doull wear at Carlton before changing his famous number eleven?
7   Ron Barassi wore number 31 in all of his 254 games for Melbourne and Carlton except for one occasion, the 1958 Grand Final. What other number did he wear on this day?
8   Leigh Matthews wore two numbers during his illustrious career with Hawthorn. What were they?
9   Geoff 'Joffa' Cunningham played 224 games for St Kilda. In 1980, he relinquished jumper number 25 and wore number 5 instead. Who took over number 25?
10 Brownlow medallist Len Thompson wore numbers 28, 3, 2 and 1 at Collingwood. What number did he wear when he played his last game with Fitzroy?

Answers

1   *Fourteen.*
2   *Gary Malarkey.*
3   *1958.*
4   *Four: Justin Madden (Essendon/Carlton), Shane Kerrison (Collingwood), John Platten (Hawthorn), and Richard Osborne (Fitzroy, Sydney and Footscray).*
5   *1912.*
6   *Number 4.*
7   *Number 2.*
8   *Numbers 32 and 3.*
9   *Alex Jesaulenko ('Jezza's' famous number at Carlton).*
10 *Number 25.*

GUERNSEY NUMBERS OF BROWNLOW WINNERS

Year	Name	Club	No.
1924	Greeves, E 'Carji'	Geelong	20
1925	Watson, Colin	St Kilda	31
1926	Warne Smith, Ivor	Melbourne	14
1927	Coventry, Syd	Collingwood	7
1928	Warne Smith, Ivor	Melbourne	14
1929	Collier, Albert	Collingwood	5
1930	Judkins, Stan	Richmond	6
	Hopkins, Allan	Footscray	1
	Collier, Harry	Collingwood	7
1931	Bunton, Haydn	Fitzroy	7
1932	Bunton, Haydn	Fitzroy	7
1933	Smallhorn, W 'Chicken'	Fitzroy	21
1934	Reynolds, Dick	Essendon	3
1935	Bunton, Haydn	Fitzroy	7
1936	Ryan, Dinny	Fitzroy	4
1937	Reynolds, Dick	Essendon	3
1938	Reynolds, Dick	Essendon	3
1939	Whelan, Marcus	Collingwood	28
1940	Fothergill, Des	Collingwood	6
	Matthews, Herbie	South Melbourne	1
1941	Ware, Norman	Footscray	4
Awards suspended during WW2 — 1942–1945			
1946	Cordner, Don	Melbourne	21
1947	Deacon, Bert	Carlton	23
1948	Morris, William (Bill)	Richmond	5
1949	Clegg, Ron	South Melbourne	23
	Austen Col	Hawthorn	9
1950	Ruthven, Alan	Fitzroy	7
1951	Smith, Bernie	Geelong	11
1952	Wright, Roy	Richmond	2
	Hutchison, Bill	Essendon	7
1953	Hutchison, Bill	Essendon	7
1954	Wright, Roy	Richmond	2
1955	Goldsmith, Fred	South Melbourne	2
1956	Box, Peter	Footscray	5
1957	Gleeson, Brian	St Kilda	30
1958	Roberts, Neil	St Kilda	10
1959	Skilton, Bob	South Melbourne	14
	Howell, Verdun	St Kilda	16
1960	Schultz, John	Footscray	14
1961	James, John	Carlton	10
1962	Lord, Alistair	Geelong	4
1963	Skilton, Bob	South Melbourne	14
1964	Collis, Gordon	Carlton	17

GUERNSEY NUMBERS OF BROWNLOW WINNERS (cont.)

Year	Name	Club	No.
1965	Stewart, Ian	St Kilda	5
	Teasdale, Noel	North Melbourne	2
1966	Stewart, Ian	St Kilda	5
1967	Smith, Ross	St Kilda	3
1968	Skilton, Bob	South Melbourne	14
1969	Murray, Kevin	Fitzroy	1
1970	Bedford, Peter	South Melbourne	11
1971	Stewart, Ian	Richmond	2
1972	Thompson, Len	Collingwood	3
1973	Greig, Keith	North Melbourne	27
1974	Greig, Keith	North Melbourne	27
1975	Dempsey, Gary	Footscray	24
1976	Moss, Graham	Essendon	25
1977	Teasedale, Graham	South Melbourne	20
1978	Blight, Malcolm	North Melbourne	15
1979	Moore, Peter	Collingwood	30
1980	Templeton, Kelvin	Footscray	31
1981	Quinlan, Bernie	Fitzroy	5
	Round, Barry	South Melbourne	25
1982	Wilson, Brian	Melbourne	7
1983	Glendinning, Ross	North Melbourne	4
1984	Moore, Peter	Melbourne	30
1985	Hardie, Brad	Footscray	4
1986	DiPierdomenico, Robert	Hawthorn	9
	Williams, Greg	Sydney	2
1987	Lockett, Tony	St Kilda	14
	Platten, John	Hawthorn	44
1988	Healy, Gerard	Sydney	3
1989	Couch, Paul	Geelong	7
1990	Liberatore, Tony	Footscray	39
1991	Stynes, Jim	Melbourne	11
1992	Wynd, Scott	Footscray	15
1993	Wanganeen, Gavin	Essendon	4
1994	Williams, Greg	Carlton	2

GUERNSEY NUMBERS OF GOALKICKERS

No.	Name	Team	Seasons	Goals kicked
1	Clover, Horrie	Carlton	1920-24 1926-31	398
2	Collins, Jack	Footscray	1950-58	385
3	Matthews, Leigh	Hawthorn	1972-85	842
4	Smith, Norm	Melbourne Fitzroy	1935-48 1948-50	572
5	Ablett, Gary	Geelong	1984-94	830
6	McKenna, Peter	Collingwood	1965-75	833
7	White, Lindsay	South Melbourne Geelong	1942-43 1944-50	475
8	Roach, Michael	Richmond	1977-89	607
9	Taylor, Brian	Collingwood	1985-90	371
10	Mohr, Bill	St Kilda	1929-41	736
11	Bedford, Peter	South Melbourne	1968-76	327
12	Titus, Jack	Richmond	1926-43	970
13	Lee, Dick	Collingwood	1914-22	420
14	Skilton, Bob	South Melbourne	1956-68 1970-71	412
15	Blight, Malcolm	North Melbourne	1974-82	445
16	Johnson, Bob	Melbourne	1926-32	420
17	Dyer, Jack	Richmond	1931-49	440
18	Beasley, Simon	Footscray	1982-89	575
19	Dunstall, Jason	Hawthorn	1985-94	1011
20	Harris, Dick	Richmond	1934-44	550
21	Morwood, Tony	South Melbourne	1978-89	398
22	Vallence, Harry	Carlton	1926-38	722
23	Wade, Doug	Geelong	1961-72	834
24	Poulter, Ray	Richmond	1946-56	345
25	Jesaulenko, Alex	Carlton St Kilda	1967-79 1980-81	444
26	Hudson, Peter	Hawthorn	1967-74	617
27	Madden, Simon	Essendon	1974-92	575
28	Wood, Bill	Footscray	1944 1946-51	284
29	Bartlett, Kevin	Richmond	1965-83	778
30	Moore, Peter	Collingwood Melbourne	1974-82 1984-87	219
31	Templeton, Kelvin	Footscray Melbourne	1974-82 1983-85	593
32	Watson, Tim	Essendon	1977-91 1993-94	337
33	Cloke, David	Richmond Collingwood	1974-82 1983-89	312
34	McGuane, Michael	Collingwood	1987-94	112

GUERNSEY NUMBERS OF GOALKICKERS (cont).

35	Daicos, Peter	Collingwood	1979-93	549
36	Maclure, Mark	Carlton	1974-86	327
37				
38	Harris, Leon	Fitzroy	1979-89	99
39	Capper, Warwick	Sydney	1983-87 1991	388
		Brisbane	1988-90	
40	Nankervis, Ian	Geelong	1967-83	203
41				
42	Walls, Robert	Carlton	1967-78	368
43	McKay, David	Carlon	1969-81	272
44	Osborne, Richard	Fitzroy	1982-92	482
		Sydney	1993	
		Footscray	1994	

PLAYERS WEARING PARTICULAR GUERNSEY NUMBERS IN THE MOST MATCHES 1897–1994

No.	Name	Team	Seasons	Matches
1	Roos, Paul	Fitzroy	1982-94	269
2	Nicholls, John	Carlton	1957-74	328
3	Whitten, Ted	Footscray	1951-70	321
4	Smith, Norm	Melbourne	1935-48	231
		Fitzroy	1949-50	
5	Rantall, John	South Melbourne	1963-72 1978-79	330
		North Melbourne	1973-75	
6	Dugdale, Joh	North Melbourne	1955-70	248
7	Hawkins, Doug	Footscray	1978-94	328
8	Clay, Dick	Richmond	1966-76	213
9	Dixon, Brian	Melbourne	1954-68	251
10	Ditterich, Carl	St Kilda	1963-72 1976-78	285
		Melbourne	1973-75 1979-80	
11	Doull, Bruce	Carlton	1972-86	332
12	Titus, Jack	Richmond	1926-43	294
13	Carter, Rod	Sydney	1980-90	217
13	Law, John	North Melbourne	1978-89	217
14	Skilton, Bob	South Melbourne	1956-68 1970-71	237
15	Moore, Kelvin	Hawthorn	1970-84	300
16	Wallace, Terry	Hawthorn	1978-86	255
		Richmond	1987	
		Footscray	1988-91	
17	Tuck, Michael	Hawthorn	1972-91	426

PLAYERS WEARING PARTICULAR GUERNSEY NUMBERS
(cont.)

18	Curcio, Frank	Fitzroy	1932-36	249
			1938-43	
			1945-48	
19	Todd, Jocka	Geelong	1922-34	232
20	Schimmelbusch, Wayne	North Melbourne	1973-87	306
21	Fletcher, Ken	Essendon	1967-80	264
22	Shaw, Tony	Collingwood	1979-94	308
23	Scott, Don	Hawthorn	1967-81	302
24	Dempsey, Gary	Footscray	1967-78	332
		North Melbourne	1979-84	
25	Jesaulenko, Alex	Carlton	1967-79	279
		St Kilda	1980-81	
26	Eade, Rodney	Hawthorn	1976-87	259
		Brisbane	1988-90	
27	Madden, Simon	Essendon	1974-92	378
28	Jones, Peter	Carlton	1968-79	249
29	Bartlett, Kevin	Richmond	1965-83	403
30	Bourke, Francis	Richmond	1967-81	300
31	Barassi, Ron	Melbourne	1953-64	253
		Carlton	1965-69	
32	Watson, Tim	Essendon	1977-91	307
			1993-94	
33	Cloke, David	Richmond	1974-82	290
		Collingwood	1983-89	
34	Kennedy, John	Hawthorn	1979-91	241
35	Daicos, Peter	Collingwood	1979-93	250
36	Maclure, Mark	Carlton	1974-86	243
37	Harmes, Wayne	Carlton	1977-86	169
			1988	
38	Harris, Leon	Fitzroy	1979-89	186
39	Higgins, Kevin	Geelong	1972-78	125
40	Nankervis, Ian	Geelong	1967-83	325
41	Rohde, Peter	Carlton	1985-87	154
		Melbourne	1988-94	
42	Walls, Robert	Carlton	1967-78	219
43	McKay, David	Carlton	1969-81	263
44	Madden, Justin	Essendon	1980-82	286
		Carlton	1983-94	
45	Ford, Michael	Footscray	1984-89	98
		St Kilda	1992	
46				
47	Jarrot, Alan	North Melbourne	1977-81	170
		Melbourne	1982-86	
48				
49	Cordy, Brian	Footscray	1981-88	124
50				
51	McLean, Michael	Footscray	1983-89	95

Did You Know?

Who were the brothers who, on the same day, made their League debut in the same game, but as opponents? Could you imagine your team standing to attention and singing 'God Save the Queen'? Who was the quickest goalkicker to reach a century? Is it legal to form a human pyramid in an effort to block a goal? Could you coach a League club and not win a game, and how long does it take to play 47 games? Football is full of such trivia.

The Jarman brothers, Andrew and Darren, created League history when they both made their AFL debuts on the same day in opposing sides. Andrew lined-up for Adelaide and Darren for Hawthorn; both played in the opening game of the 1991 season at Football Park.

Other brothers to make their League debuts on the same day include Phil and Ted Ryan. Phil, who later became President of Hawthorn, made his League debut in 1941 playing for Hawthorn, while on the same day brother Ted stripped for Collingwood. Jim and Phil Krakouer also made their League debuts on the same day, playing for North Melbourne, in 1982 in the opening round against Richmond.

• • •

In 1935, umpire Bill Blackburn experienced a dog of a day. During play in the match between Carlton and Collingwood at Princes Park, an aggressive canine upset players so much that Blackburn stopped the game to catch it. As he was putting it over the fence, he was severely bitten on the hand.

• • •

During the second quarter of a spiteful match at Princes Park in 1924, St Kilda skipper Welles Eicke commented that Carlton had 19 men on the field. The field umpire halted play and lined the Blues up for a count. As he informed Eicke that the claim was unfounded, a voice was heard to remark sarcastically, 'You didn't count yourself.'

• • •

All but four of Carlton's selected team travelled by train to play Geelong at Corio Oval in 1918. The quartet decided to make the journey by motor car. Unfortunately, tyre trouble caused a lengthy delay. A car finally raced into the carpark as the Blues ran onto the field at 2.15 pm, but the occupants were unimpressed to find the selection committee had called in last minute replacements.

• • •

At the end of the half-time break in the match between Carlton and Essendon at the East Melbourne Cricket Ground on Wednesday 23 May 1900, both teams assembled in front of the pavilion to sing 'God Save the Queen' to celebrate a major victory in the Boer War in South Africa. A public holiday had been declared, and the League match was hastily re-scheduled because heavy rain had made play impossible on the previous Saturday.

• • •

During the 1960s and '70s, several players made spectacles of themselves. Geoff Blethyn and Rod McFarlane, both of Essendon; Jim Wright, Geelong; Bruce Brown, Melbourne and Essendon; and Tony Southcombe, Carlton, all wore glasses on the field. St Kilda's Chris Stone also wore squash glasses to protect a previous eye injury.

• • •

Sid Dockendorf played 13 matches for Richmond in 1932 and 1933, before moving to Fitzroy in 1935 where he eventually became captain. During his time at Tigerland, he became an almost permanent bench-warmer. He assumed the 19th-man role on ten occasions, six of which were consecutive. One wonders how many splinters he acquired and how many dressing gowns he wore out.

• • •

Ernest 'Bung' Newling possessed an unusual nickname. The courageous Geelong halfback gave excellent service in 150 matches during an eleven-season career which began in 1900. He displayed great concentration, speed and cleverness, despite the fact that he possessed sight in only one eye — hence the nickname 'Bung-eyed Newling'.

• • •

Jim Jackson made his League debut with St Kilda in Round 2 of 1909 against Collingwood at the Junction Oval. That was to be his only appearance with the Saints. He transferred to the Magpies a year later where he played 93 matches before bidding farewell to Victoria Park in 1920. In 1925, he was appointed captain of Hawthorn in its first VFL season. Round 8 of the season was a special day for him when he led his team against Essendon at Glenferrie Oval. He was making his 100th League appearance. The milestone had taken an amazing 16 years and 43 days, more than twelve years longer than Glen Jakovich of the West Coast Eagles had spent in achieving the same feat (Jakovich played 100 games of League football in a shorter space of time than anyone else—four years and 22 days). Jackson finally retired after the 1926 season.

• • •

Essendon champion ruckman Simon Madden began his 19-season career as a 16-year-old in 1974. His 378 matches and 575 goals are the most by a natural left-footer in League history. It is estimated that less than ten per cent of the football population prefers the left foot. Five natural left-footers have worn particular guernsey numbers more often than anyone else in League history: Number 9, Brian Dixon of Melbourne, 251 matches; number 14, Bob Skilton, South Melbourne, 237 matches; number 22, Tony Shaw, Collingwood, 308 matches; number 39, Kevin Higgins, Geelong, 125 matches; and number 44, Justin Madden, Essendon and Carlton, 286 matches.

• • •

The first League match played at night for premiership points took place on Monday 16 June 1952 as part of the special promotion when all matches were played outside the Melbourne/Geelong area. In front of almost 30 000 people, Essendon defeated Geelong convincingly at the floodlit Brisbane Exhibition Ground. Bomber champion John Coleman starred with thirteen goals.

• • •

Currently, footy fans are treated to extensive electronic and print media coverage of AFL matches. Radio coverage reached amazing heights in 1961 and 1962 when eight stations provided descriptions every Saturday. In 1965 and 1966, all four Melbourne TV channels showed an hour of replays commencing at 6pm on match days.

• • •

In 1957, the three existing Melbourne TV stations reached an agreement with the VFL to telecast matches for the first time. In return for a weekly fee of £50 ($100), each channel was permitted to show a live coverage of the last quarter of any match.

• • •

One of Fitzroy's toughest and most durable players was Frank Curcio who accumulated 249 matches in a career spanning from 1932 until 1948. In contrast to his steamrolling tactics on Saturday afternoons, he made a living as a professional violinist. No opponent dared to fiddle with him on the field!

• • •

The legendary Roy Cazaly played 99 matches for St Kilda from 1910 until 1920. He added exactly the same number of games to his career as a South Melbourne champion between 1921 and 1927. The song 'Up There, Cazaly' became a national hit and an AFL anthem.

• • •

In 1924 Fitzroy recruited Essendon discard Jack Moriarty. The 'Dons must have had second thoughts about their generosity when he scored seven goals in each of his first three matches for the Brunswick Street team. He gave Fitzroy great service, accumulating 626 goals in 157 games. In his only season with Essendon in 1922, he booted a respectable 36 goals in thirteen matches.

• • •

Bert Hurrey was a quick, clever, versatile player from 1908 until 1913. He was the only player to register a century for University who competed in 126 League matches between 1908 and 1914. Hurrey participated in 101 of those games and booted 29 goals before moving to South Australia after completing a course in medicine.

• • •

An old rule which permitted any number of players to stand on the mark led to an amazing finish in a match between Geelong and Fitzroy in 1924. Eric Fleming of Geelong marked near goal right on the bell with his side trailing by three points. To Fleming's amazement, three Fitzroy backmen built themselves into a pyramid on his mark. Despite these acrobatic efforts, Fleming goaled to win the game for Geelong, and the rule was swiftly revised.

• • •

Round 8 of the 1992 AFL season was one of the great football promotions. The game of the century, marking 100 years to the day since Collingwood's first game as a senior club in the League, took place on a Thursday night under lights at the MCG against traditional enemy Carlton. The match was preceded by a motorcade of former great players and a spectacular fireworks display, and 83 262 fanatical fans were treated to a game played with the intensity of a grand final. Unfortunately for Collingwood, Carlton returned the result of 100 years before, winning 16 goals 9 (105) points to 9 goals 18 (72). For Carlton, it was their 100th League victory since 1897 at the MCG, and the Blues skipper Stephen Kernahan capped a great game by booting 7 goals 1.

• • •

Round 15 of the 1989 season saw history created at Carrara, the home of the Brisbane Bears. The lights were turned on there for the first time for the game between the Bears and Geelong. More than 18 000 fans turned out for a spectacular evening. The ground boasted six light towers producing lighting similar to the MCG and the SCG at a cost of $5 million. Unfortunately for the Bears, Geelong spoilt the party and handed out a 70-point defeat to the home side. The Cats kicked 12 goals 6 in the final term, the highest score in one quarter in the club's history. After the game, Brisbane coach Peter Knights was sacked and replaced by former North Melbourne and Richmond player Paul Feltham.

• • •

Round 21 of the 1971 season between Fitzroy and Carlton at the Junction Oval will always be known as the day of the fog. Just after half-time a blanket of fog swept over the ground making play near impossible as visibility was down to a few yards. Field umpire Bill Deller had to rely on an emergency umpire relaying to him what score had been kicked, as he could not see the goal umpires. Legend has it that from a Carlton kick-in, Blues ruckman Percy Jones caught sight of the ball and yelled 'There it is!' — and a Fitzroy player picked it up and kicked a goal! The Lions won the game by 21 points, and Carlton missed the finals.

• • •

When it comes to kicking a football, St Kilda's Dave McNamara is still considered the daddy of them all. His long kicking left spectators of his era speechless. McNamara had an interrupted career that started in 1905 and finished in 1923. In the record books, he is credited with kicking the ball 79 metres (86 yards one foot) at Launceston in 1913, and 85 metres (93 yards) in a match against Geelong in 1923. McNamara once said his one regret was he never kicked the ball 91.5 metres (one hundred yards). Despite his skills in all departments, McNamara's fame rests with the now forgotten art of place kicking.

• • •

The week leading up to the final home and away game of the 1992 season centred around Essendon and its coach Kevin Sheedy. The football world wondered whether Sheedy would bring back into the senior team his two great old champions — Simon Madden and Terry Daniher — for their last game of senior football. Both players had been relegated to kicking the dew off the ground in the Reserves and the pressure was on Sheedy to give his former stars one final game to end their outstanding careers. Sure enough, when the side was announced to play Geelong, there was Madden and Daniher in the line-up, and Sheedy had shown there was still some sentiment left in football. Both players ran a lap of honour before the game, but Geelong spoilt the party by downing the Bombers by 46 points. Between them, Madden and Daniher had played 692 games and kicked 1046 goals.

• • •

Few AFL clubs have experienced such a non-success period as Fitzroy during the 1963 and '64 seasons. During those dark years the Lions could only manage one win, that being in 1963 and a monumental upset over Geelong, who went on to win the premiership that year. The following year, Fitzroy lost every game, coming agonisingly close on two occasions, only to lose to Carlton and North Melbourne by a point.

• • •

The biggest headlines of 1982 centred around the move of South Melbourne to Sydney. The name South Melbourne was dropped, and the club became known as the Swans, and played eleven home games at the SCG. The launch of the Swans took place at the Sydney Opera House, and AFL President Dr Allen Aylett said the preparation had been done and now it was up to the players. The captain of the Swans at that historic moment in the club's history was Barry Round, and the coach, former player Ricky Quade.

• • •

The 1983 season produced one of the biggest news stories in the history of the AFL. Silvio Foschini threw the AFL rules and regulations into turmoil when he won a restraint of trade case in course. Foschini wanted a clearance from the Swans to St Kilda, and the court ruled that he had been given a permit to play for the Saints. On the afternoon Foschini made his debut for the Saints, the St Kilda hierarchy also decided to play Swans player Paul Morwood without a clearance. Chief Justice Crockett on 15 April held that the AFL's rules and regulations were in restraint of trade. After an extensive overhaul, new AFL regulations were adopted by the AFL board.

• • •

League football has been played in the morning only on two occasions. The first occasion was to celebrate the visit of His Royal Highness the Prince of Wales to Melbourne in 1920. Richmond and Collingwood slugged it out at Punt Road with the Tigers winning by seven points, and Fitzroy accounted for Geelong easily by 40 points. Then in 1938 the League experimented with a before-noon start when Essendon downed St Kilda.

• • •

Bouncing the ball to start a game is a unique part of League football. The ball was originally thrown up to start games, but in 1887 the bounce was introduced. It was another four years before the umpire bounced the ball in the centre of the ground after a goal had been scored.

• • •

Around 1880, Essendon and Melbourne were the two clubs that forced the introduction of players wearing white shorts. Supporters had difficulty in picking out players due to the similar colours of the jumpers. In 1924 black shorts were introduced for the home team with the away side wearing white. Today the home side can wear shorts in the club colours.

• • •

It wasn't until 1964 that the League allowed coaches to talk to their charges at quarter time. Before that, teams used to just change ends on the siren and the games resumed when players were in position. In 1978, the 19th and 20th man was replaced by the interchange system that allowed players to be rotated on and off the ground.

• • •

VFL games were first shown on television in 1957. Tony Charlton (HSV7), Ken Dakin (ABC) and Ian Johnson (GTV 9) were the commentators. A direct telecast of the final terms was permitted. In 1961, stations showed a one-hour replay programme. When Queen Elizabeth visited Australia in 1970, Her Highness was a special guest at the match between Fitzroy and Richmond at the MCG. This game was televised live. In 1977, Channel 7 had a direct telecast of the grand final between Collingwood and North Melbourne after the match was a sell-out. The game ended in a draw, and Channel 7 again televised the match direct. The replay was won by North.

• • •

It wasn't until 1956 that League coaches were able to use a runner to deliver their messages to players. Acting on reports that clubs were abusing the privilege and more than one person was being used, the League in 1965 designated that only one registered runner was able to carry the coach's instructions while the game was in progress.

• Quick Quiz •

1   Who wore glasses in the 1968 Grand Final?

2   Name the three teams that entered the VFL in 1925.

3   Which team is sometimes referred to as the Redlegs?

4   Who won West Coast's first ever best and fairest award in 1987?

5   Who coached Sydney in between Gary Buckenara being sacked and Ron Barassi taking over during the 1993 season?

6   Which club scored a total of one point in a match against Geelong in 1899?

7   How many venues have hosted League matches for premiership points since the formation of the VFL/AFL?

8   Which club was defeated by Adelaide in the first League match at Football Park?

9   Name the club which was once known as the Mustard Pots?

10 In which season was the two-field-umpire system first used in League matches?

Answers

1   *Geoff Blethyn (Essendon).*
2   *Hawthorn, Footscray and North Melbourne.*
3   *Melbourne.*
4   *Steve Malaxos.*
5   *Brett Scott.*
6   *St Kilda.*
7   *32.*
8   *Hawthorn.*
9   *Hawthorn.*
10 *1976.*

And the Big Men Fly...

Marking is the most spectacular aspect of Australian Rules football. The highflyers have thrilled the fans since the days of Dick Lee, the great Collingwood full-forward in the early 1900s.

Taking the 'specky' is the dream of every kid running around in the park, and the memories we have of some of the game's greats centre around their marking capabilities. South Melbourne legend Bob Pratt, the first player to kick 150 goals in League football, based his game around spectacular high marks. Essendon great John Coleman had the turnstiles ticking over from his first game and 13 goals in 1949. The fans wanted to see his phenomenal marking feats. Another South Melbourne great, Roy Cazaly, inspired 'Up There Cazaly', our game's most recognizable song, which immortalised his ability to jump. Alex Jesaulenko, apart from being one of the all-time greats, will always be remembered for his death-defying leap onto the back of Graeme 'Jerker' Jenkin (Collingwood) when playing for Carlton in the 1970 Grand Final. And arguments continue as to whether there has ever been a more freakish mark than the one taken by Peter Bosustow (Carlton, 1981–83) against Geelong at Princes Park. Legend has it that before the game the 'Buzz' predicted he would take the mark of the year.

In 1979, I was at ground level when Michael Roach (Richmond) took the mark of the year over Kelvin and Terry Moore (Hawthorn). I strained my neck just looking up at Roach as he came back out of the clouds. And, of course, in recent years Geelong champ Gary Ablett has thrilled the football public with some of the greatest marks the game has seen. Marking is a spontanious action guaranteed to get the fans out of their seats.

Page 168: Former Carlton champion Alex Jesaulenko takes one of many spectacular marks — this time over Collingwood's Graeme 'Jerker' Jenkin in the 1970 Grand Final. Sergio Silvagni, father of Stephen, looks on. (Spider Funnell/Sporting Pix)

• • •

Page 169: Kevin Bartlett looks on as Richmond forward Michael Roach takes a brilliant mark in a match against Hawthorn at the MCG played in Round 5 of the 1979 season. (Alan Funnel/Sporting Pix)

• • •

Page 170: Playing for Carlton, Peter Bosustow flys high against Geelong in Round 18 of the 1981 season. (VFL Archives/Sporting Pix)

• • •

Page 171: Geelong's Gary Ablett climbs above the pack to take another trademark grab, playing against Melbourne at the MCG in 1989. (John Krutop/Sporting Pix)

• • •

Page 172: Warwick Capper, former high-marking forward for the Sydney Swans, showed his great aerial skills when he took this mark over a Richmond opponent back in 1991. (Ken Rainsbury/Sport. The Library)

• • •

Page 173: Chris Waterman takes a diving mark for the West Coast Eagles over Wayne Carey and Glen Jakovich in the 1993 Second Elimination Final against North Melbourne. (John Daniels/Sporting Pix)

• • •

Page 174: For once Gary Ablett's feet remain firmly on the ground as teammate Billy Brownless takes a screamer over Ashley McIntosh in the 1994 Grand Final. (Tony Feder/Sporting Pix)

Acknowledgements

The Author and the Publishers express their thanks
to the following:

Sporting Pix, for permission to reproduce all
photographs in the text and on the front cover
(with the exception of the photograph of
Warwick Capper on page *172*)

•

Sport: The Library, for permission to reproduce the
photograph of Warwick Capper on page *172*

•

Jim Stirling, for permission to use the photograph of
Kevin Bartlett that appears on the back cover
of the book

•

Colin Hutchinson, for his assistance and meticulous
research

•

Danny Finley, of Raceplay the Sporting Company,
for his support, enthusiasm, and contributions
to the book

•

Andrew Adam, for his support and assistance in
proofreading the football stories.

•

The Five Mile Press

The Five Mile Press Pty Ltd
22 Summit Road
Noble Park Victoria 3174
Australia

First published 1995

Editor: Emma Borghesi
Statistics editor: Emma Short
Editorial and production assistant: Robyn Ambrose
Statistics formatting: Digitype
Cover design: Peter Bourne

Printed in Australia

National Library of Australia
Cataloguing in Publication Data:
Bartlett, Kevin
Kevin Bartlett's book of football
ISBN 0 86788 982 9 (Pbk.)
1. Australian football - Anecdotes. 2. Australian football - Miscellanea.
I. Title. II. Title: Book of football.
796.336.